The Epistles of John
Through New Eyes
From Behind the Veil

Peter J. Leithart

Athanasius
Press

Monroe, Louisiana

The Epistles of John Through New Eyes: *From Behind the Veil*
Copyright © 2009 by Athanasius Press
205 Roselawn
Monroe, Louisiana 71201
www.athanasiuspress.org

ISBN: 978-0-9842439-0-7 (softcover)

CONTENTS

1

THE LAST HOUR

1 John is not like Galatians, where Paul tells us emphatically what the Galatians have done to provoke his stern letter. It is not like 1 Corinthians where, again, Paul addresses explicit questions and problems in the Corinthian church. John[1] does not give us any

---

1. From the early centuries, the church has attributed these three short letters to John the son of Zebedee, the brother of James, and the author of the fourth gospel. Apart from the testimony of the early church, the main support for this identification is the similarity of the letter and the gospel, which are considerable. Both the gospel and the first epistle begin with the phrase "in the beginning" (John 1:1; 1 John 1:1), and in both works the author explains the gospel in the same terms: the "only-begotten" (John 1:14, 18; 3:16; 1 John 4:9) Word that was in the beginning came in flesh (John 1:14; 1 John 4:2), and "laid down his life" for us (John 10:11–18; 1 John 3:16) so that we might "have life" (John 3:15; 1 John 5:11). Of course, it has often been doubted that John ben Zebedee wrote the fourth gospel, but I am persuaded that the traditional identification of John as the author is perfectly plausible. In 2 John, John identifies himself, not as an apostle but as an

overt description of the problem he's addressing, and doesn't even tell us who his audience is. For this reason, scholars have long classified 1 John among the "Catholic" or "universal" epistles.

From the letter itself, however, we can see that the churches John writes to are in crisis. They are fighting off false teachers who deny central Christian truths, and they are living in what John calls the "last hour." John's letters were not written in the leisure of a seminary office; they are letters of exhortation, encouragement, warning, and rebuke. John writes into a specific pastoral situation: can we reconstruct it?

1–3 JOHN IN THE NEW TESTAMENT CANON

The gospel goes to the Jew first. When they resist, Paul turns to the Gentiles, but he hopes by this to provoke the Jews to jealousy, so that in the end Jews will be saved along with Gentiles (Rom. 9–11). In the New Testament, the gospel moves from Jew to Gentile and back (in hope) to Jew.

The New Testament canon, arguably, does something similar.[2] The order of the canon expresses both the basic structure of New

---

elder. The word "elder" (Greek *presbuteros*, from which we derive our term "presbyterian") basically means "someone who is old," but in ancient Israel and in the early church, the term came to be used for an office or authority, rule, and judgment. The "elder" may not be "older" in a literal, chronological sense, but he must be "older" in his faithfulness, more mature, more advanced in his life as a believer. Would an apostle such as John identify himself as an "elder"? Peter does (1 Pet. 5:1), and therefore it is possible that John would as well. The two terms refer to two different aspects of John's ministry. As apostle, John is commissioned with the authority of Jesus to preach and act in Jesus' name; as elder, John is a respected mature man in the Christian community. In this commentary, I assume that John ben Zebedee is the author of both the gospel and the first epistle, and that he is likewise the "elder" who addresses the "lady" in 2 John and 3 John. That means that John wrote a large portion of the New Testament. He received the revelation of the Apocalypse from Jesus; he wrote a gospel; and he wrote three epistles.

2. I came to the following conclusions through a series of very stimulating conversations with my student Molly Miltenberger.

Testament history and basic premises of New Testament theology. Initially, the gospels focus on Jesus' work among the lost sheep of the house of Israel. Though he has occasional contact with Gentiles, his primary ministry is to Jews. Acts begins in Jerusalem, but ends in Rome with Paul turning from the Roman Jews to Gentiles. Turn the page, and Paul is writing to Christians in Rome, a neat epistolary continuation of Acts, and the remainder of Paul's letters are addressed to Christians in Gentile areas and to what are partly (if not predominantly) Gentile churches. If Hebrews is Pauline, it marks a shift in focus, a canonical replication of Paul's argument in Romans 9–11: having ministered among the Gentiles, he is now trying to win his brothers according to the flesh. (Hebrews also makes a neat numerological conclusion to a Pauline corpus—14 letters.)

Following the Pauline letters, the Catholic epistles continue the trend of Hebrews, being epistles to Jewish believers. James addresses the "twelve tribes dispersed abroad" (1:1; Greek *diaspora*). This does not, I have argued elsewhere, refer to the *diaspora* of Jews in general, but specifically to the *diaspora* of Christian Jews following the outbreak of persecution after the stoning of Stephen (see Acts 8:1ff, with its *diaspora* language).[3] Even if I am wrong in that conclusion, it remains the case that James writes to Jews, or to people imagined as Jews. Peter does the same, addressing the believers who have been "scattered" (*diaspora*) from Jerusalem (1 Pet. 1:1). If, as seems to be the case (2 Pet. 3:1), 2 Peter is addressed to the same audience as 1 Peter, it too addresses these Jewish-Christian aliens. Revelation is the capstone, a final letter from Jesus to his people in Jerusalem.[4]

Like the Pauline epistles (if Hebrews is included), the Catholic epistles have a numerological structure as well: seven "Catholic" epistles (perhaps "General Hebraic" would be a better description),

---

3. *The Promise of His Appearing: An Exposition of 2 Peter* (Moscow, ID: Canon Press, 2004).

4. On Revelation, see James B. Jordan, *A Reader's Guide to Revelation* (Monroe, LA: Athanasius Press, 2008).

then the seven letters to the churches of Asia minor (Rev. 1–3), and the "eighth" letter in Revelation, the big, long letter, sent to the Harlot Jerusalem warning of her impending doom (Rev. 4–22). Along the way, thousands of Jews turn to Jesus, and the Bible ends with new creation emerging from the destruction of the great city.

I suggest the following narrative and redemptive-historical logic for the organization of the New Testament canon:

Books	Focus
Gospels	Jews[5]
Pauline	Gentiles, turning to Jews
Catholic	Jews
Revelation	End of Jerusalem

Within that setting, John's letters are part of the New Testament's final response to Judaism. They are part of the last-ditch New Testament address to Israel and the problems surrounding Israel's unbelief. If this speculation about the design of the canon is valid, then it provides general guidelines for understanding the setting and circumstances of John's letters. During the Pauline phase of first-century history, the ministry of the church turned to the Gentiles, but John's epistles are part of a climactic confrontation with Judaism, overshadowed by the promise that "all Israel will be saved." Is this canonical speculation borne out by the contents of the letters?

HISTORICAL SETTING

In several phrases, John provides clues about the timing of his letters. He writes in "the last hour" (2:18), at a time when "the world is passing away" (2:17). That the world is coming to an end is evident from the "antichrists" (2:18) who have already appeared in the

---

5. The gospels introduce a complexity, anticipating the movement from Jew to Gentile to Jew. Matthew is addressed to a Jewish audience, Mark and Luke to Gentiles, but John turns his attention back to the problem of Judaism. The gospels thus form a miniature of the entire New Testament canon.

world (4:3). Many Christians believe that John is talking about the end of the physical universe, but if so, he is, obviously, wrong. Two thousand years on, the physical universe has not passed away and John's lifetime was not the "last hour" of human history. John is instead talking about the end of the old order, which Jesus predicted at length (Matt. 24; Mark 13; Luke 21) and which John himself saw in the visions of Revelation. John means that the Old Covenant order—with its temple, priesthood, sacrifices, and rules of cleanliness—is coming to its end, and soon. The "last hour" is the "last hour" of the Old Covenant. That means he is writing shortly before the Roman attack on Jerusalem and the destruction of the temple, sometime in the 60s AD.

Too often, preterist interpretations of the New Testament focus only on the destruction of the temple and city of Jerusalem, but the New Testament's sights are broader.[6] From the time of the Babylonian exile, Yahweh placed Israel in the midst of a series of Gentile empires (Babylon, Persia, Greece, Rome; cf. Daniel 2; 7). With the destruction of the temple, the Lord ended not only the old order centered on Jerusalem but the old world-system that had existed since the time of Nebuchadnezzar. After 70 AD, Rome retained its empire for several centuries in the West and for over a millennium in the East, but its role as the Gentile "guardian" of Israel ended in the first century. When John says that the world is "passing away," he is talking about the late antique geo-political order.

However, John means even more than that. As we'll see below, John proclaims the good news that the period of the Lord's absence, his hiding and secrecy, has come to an end. He has manifested himself in flesh. Before the coming of Jesus, both Jew and Gentile lived under the "elementary principles" of the world (*stoicheia*; cf. Gal. 4:1–11). Jews and Gentiles were under a regime of prohibition and taboo that was cultural, religious, and political, all

---

6. These reflections are dependent on various writings of James Jordan, most recently and fully in *The Handwriting on the Wall: A Commentary on the Book of Daniel* (Atlanta: American Vision, 2007).

at once. John announces that with the coming of the Word of Life, what was holy and untouchable is now touchable; the unseen is made visible. He announces the end of the whole Old Covenant order, with its regulations of "taste not, touch not, handle not."

This background helps clarify some of John's major concerns. John, for example, mentions "antichrist" several times. In 2:18, he writes, "It is the last hour, and just as you heard that antichrist is coming, even now many antichrists have arisen; from this we know that it is the last hour." Where did they hear that antichrist was coming? They perhaps heard it from John, or from another apostle or preacher. But where did the apostles learn about antichrist? If John had already received the visions recorded in Revelation, that might be one source. Ultimately, though, Jesus' own teaching is the source, especially the sermon recorded in Matthew 24 and its parallels. Early on in the discourse on the Mount of Olives, Jesus warns that "many will come in My name saying, 'I am the Christ' and will mislead many" (Matt. 24:5). Again in 24:24 he adds, "false Christs and false prophets will arise and will show great signs and wonders, so as to mislead, if possible, even the elect." Similarly, John warns about antichrists and "false prophets" (2:18–19; 4:1). John is saying that antichrist has come, just as Jesus predicted. As Jesus warned, the appearance of antichrist is a sign of the approaching end of the age.

Can we be more specific? Can we identify the specific kind of false teachers, false Christs, and false prophets threatening John's churches?

GNOSTICISM?

Many commentators on 1 John believe he is opposing an early form of Gnosticism and Docetism. Docetism comes from the Greek verb *dokeō*, which means "seem." A docetic Christology is one that teaches that Jesus was the Son of God, but not fully human. His humanity was only an "appearance," not genuine humanity. John Stott explains, "He 'seemed' to the eyes of witnesses to be truly human, but it was a disguise similar to that of the Old Testament theophanies when God (or the angel of the Lord) appeared in the form of a man."[7] This was a heresy during the early patristic period, opposed by Ignatius and Tertullian among others. John appears to refer to this false Christology when he states in 4:2 that the false teachers deny that "Jesus Christ has come in the flesh." Against the Docetists, John insists on the genuine humanity of Jesus.

In his first epistle, however, John doesn't give a great deal of emphasis to the fleshliness of Jesus. He mentions it in 4:2, and it is implicit in the opening verses of the letter, but John does not indicate that it is particularly characteristic of the false teachers' theology. One commentator has suggested that when John talks about Jesus, his emphasis is not so much on the "real humanity of Jesus" as on "the personal identity of the pre-existent Divine Christ with Jesus."[8] John is addressing a more subtle Christological error. On this view, the humanity of Jesus is real humanity, but his human nature cannot be identified as the human nature of the Son of God. There is some "space," a "buffer zone," that protects the Divine Son from too intimate contact with the human Jesus. Heretics holding to this Christology could not say, as Luther rightly did, "This man is God, this God is man."

The assumption behind this Christology, as behind the docetic Christology, is that the flesh—bodily stuff, matter—is evil, impure, defiling. It would be unworthy of God to have any kind of close contact with flesh, or, worse, God might himself be defiled if he came into close contact with low matter. That is, both of these Christologies display a gnostic view of the material world. Stott's summary is again helpful:

> Gnosticism is a broad term embracing various pagan, Jewish and semi-Christian systems, which did not come to full development until the second century. It was pagan in origin, combining elements of "Western intellectualism and Eastern mysticism"

---

7. John R. W. Stott, *The Letters of John* (Tyndale New Testament Commentaries; rev. ed.; Grand Rapids: Eerdmans, 1988), 48.

8. Quoted in Stott, *Letters*, 48.

(Law). . . . The notion that matter is inherently evil was both orien-
tal and Greek. It led to speculations about the origin of the material
universe and how it could in any sense have been created by the
Supreme Being who is good. The Gnostics posited a series of
"aeons" or emanations from the Supreme, each more removed
from him than its predecessors, until there emerged one
sufficiently remote to create the material world.[9]

Gnostics might agree that the man Jesus had a body, but they
deny that there could be any personal identification between the Son
and the human body. Stott says, "They could not conceive how the
'Christ' could have become incarnate, still less have assumed a body
subject to suffering and pain. As for the Christian's body, it was fundamental to their thought that the body was a base prison in which
the rational or spiritual part of human beings was incarcerated, and
from which it needed to be released by *gnosis*, knowledge. They believed in salvation by enlightenment. This enlightenment could
come by the imparting of an esoteric knowledge in some secret initiation ceremony."[10]

Does John appear to be responding to gnostic Christology?
John's positive teaching about Jesus is that he is "the Christ" (5:10),
that he came in the flesh (1:1–4; 4:2), that he is the Son (repeatedly),
and that he came "by water and blood" (5:6). That is a thoroughly
anti-gnostic Christology, and the church was right to cite 1 John in
later debates with Gnostics. Identifying the heretics of 1–3 John as
Gnostics gets us close to the truth, but in my judgment John's focus
is elsewhere.

What then? What false teaching are the false teachers teaching?
We can begin by asking how John defines "antichrist." In 2:22–23,
the antichrist is the one who "denies that Jesus is Messiah," and this
denial of the Son is also a denial of the Father. Though this might

9. Stott, *Letters*, 49. The "aeons" formed a buffer zone between the high God
and the creation, and gnostic Christologies simply transferred this buffer zone to
Christ.

10. Stott, *Letters*, 49.

describe gnostic Christology, it is just as accurate as a description of anti-Christian Judaism. Many Jews, obviously enough, denied that Jesus was the Messiah, the Anointed One from Yahweh. In fact, John's description of the views of antichrists applies more precisely to Jews than to anyone else. What sense does it make for a *Greek* to deny that Jesus is "Messiah"? Did they expect a Messiah in the first place? Wouldn't they simply be indifferent, as Pilate was, to the internal Jewish debates about messiahship? Further, 4:2–3 says that "every spirit that confesses that Jesus Christ has come in the flesh is from God, and every spirit that does not confess Jesus is not from God." The latter spirit, the spirit that does not confess Jesus, is the spirit of "antichrist" and the spirit of "false prophets" (4:1). While John does mention the coming of Jesus "in the flesh" here, the thing that makes antichrists anti-Christ is the fact that they refuse to confess Jesus as Christ and Lord. Again, this makes more sense as a description of Jewish unbelief than it does of "Gentile" or "Greek" Gnosticism.

John's opponents, I submit, are primarily Jews or Judaizing Christians. If this is the case, what do we make of the gnostic echoes that so many commentators have heard in the letter?

GNOSTIC AND JEW

Here is a hypothesis: Gnosticism is, in (perhaps large) part, a product of Judaism and, more specifically, of Judaizing.

On the face of it, this is a bizarre thesis. Gnosticism is a radically dualistic system, while Judaism affirms the goodness of creation from the first pages of its Bible. Counterintuitive as it may seem, several lines of evidence link Judaism and Gnosticism.

First, a substantial body of scholarly literature connects Gnosticism with various forms of Judaism.[11] The links vary. R. M. Grant

---

11. The literature is helpfully summarized in Michel Desjardins, "Judaism and Gnosticism" in *Hellization Revisited: Shaping a Christian Response within the Greco-Roman World* (ed. Wendy E. Helleman; University Press of America, 1994), 309–21. A

claims that Gnosticism arose from the crisis of Judaism after the fall of the temple in 70 AD,[12] while Carl Smith has more recently found the source of Gnosticism in the "alienated Judaism" that followed the unsuccessful revolt against Trajan from 115 to 117 AD.[13] Jarl Fossum examines Samaritan speculations about the angel of Yahweh as a source of Gnostic theories of the Demiurge.[14] Karl Rudolph found deeper roots in Judaism's apocalyptic and sapiential traditions:

> The separation of the world and God, the loss of confidence in the sense of existence . . . and the pessimism with its hedonistic and world-renouncing tendencies are the precursors to the Gnostic view of existence. God becomes a remote being who stands beyond the earthly, chaotic activities; the "unknown God" makes his appearance. The vacuum thus brought into existence between the distant, alien God and the world, connected only by the primeval act of creation, is filled by angels, spirits and demons. It only needs a final act which severs this bond as well, which attributes the senselessness and the ungodly activity of the world to a power opposed to God, while the true God remains in the unchangeable and undefiled world beyond, and the Gnostic view

---

number of the essays in Birger Pearson, *Gnosticism, Judaism, and Egyptian Christianity* (Minneapolis: Fortress, 2006), trace Gnostic interpretations of biblical texts to Jewish sources, and brief introductions to the Jewish sources of Gnosticism may be found in Pheme Perkins, "Gnosticism" in *The Encyclopedia of Early Christianity* (ed., Everett Ferguson; New York: Garland, 1990), 371–76, and Kurt Rudolph, *Gnosis* (trans. Robert McLachlan Wilson; San Francisco: Harper & Row, 1985), 275–82. See also R. McL. Wilson, "Gnostic Origins," *Vigiliae Christianae* 9:3 (1955), 193–211, and Wilson, "Gnostic Origins Again," *Vigiliae Christianae* 11:2 (1957), 93–110. The notion that Gnosticism originated from Jewish sources goes back, in recent centuries, to Moritz Friedlander's *Der vorchristliche judische Gnosticismus* (1898), whose argument Pearson summarizes in the first chapter of his book. There are skeptics: Edwin Yamauchi, *Pre-Christian Gnosticism: A Survey of Proposed Evidences* (Eugene, OR: Wipf & Stock, 2003), first published in 1973; and W. C. van Unnik, "Die judische Komponente in der entstehung der Gnosis," *Vigiliae Christianae* 15:2 (1961), 65–82.

12. Grant, *Gnosticism and Early Christianity* (New York: Columbia, 1966).

13. Carl B. Smith, *No Longer Jews: The Search for Gnostic Origins* (Hendrickson, 2004).

14. Jarl E. Fossum, *The Name of God and the Angel of the Lord: Samaritan and Jewish Concepts of Intermediation and the Origin of Gnosticism* (Wissenschaftliche Untersuchungen zum Neuen Testament #36; Mohr Siebeck, 1985).

of the world is born. For in Gnosis this God as well as the Demiurge shows traits of the Jewish God. It can therefore be said with
good reason that the skepticism which was born of doubt in the
power of divine wisdom prepared the way for Gnosis, a way
which led out from official Judaism and ended in contradiction to
it. We are then dealing with a critical self-dissolution on the
fringes of Judaism.[15]

Second, the church fathers often claim that the Samaritan con-
vert Simon Magus was the first Gnostic, the origin of the Christian
Gnostic heresy, and more generally early church writings often
trace heretical movements to Judaism. The *Apostolic Constitutions*
(6.6–7) lists heresies within Judaism, which were behind many of
the early Christian heresies:

> [F]or of them were the Sadducees, who do not confess the resur-
> rection of the dead; and the Pharisees, who ascribe the practice of
> sinners to fortune and fate; and the Basmotheans, who deny
> providence, and say that the world is made by spontaneous mo-
> tion, and take away the immortality of the soul; and the
> Hemerobaptists, who every day, unless they wash, do not eat, —
> nay, and unless they cleanse their beds and tables, or platters and
> cups and seats, do not make use of any of them; and those who
> are newly risen amongst us, the Ebionites, who will have the Son
> of God to be a mere man, begotten by human pleasure, and the
> conjunction of Joseph and Mary. There are also those that
> separate themselves from all these, and observe the laws of their
> fathers, and these are the Essenes. These, therefore, arose among
> the former people. And now the evil one, who is wise to do
> mischief, and as for goodness, knows no such good thing, has
> cast out some from among us, and has wrought by them heresies
> and schisms.

From these Jewish sects sprang various Christian heresies, beginning with Simon, a Samaritan: "Now the original of the new
heresies began thus: the devil entered into one Simon, of a village

---

15. *Gnosis*, 282.

called Gitthæ, a Samaritan, by profession a magician, and made him the minister of his wicked design."[16]

While the *Apostolic Constitutions* does not name Gnostic heresies per se, Eusebius does, and traces them to Simon. Quoting a lost work of Hegisippus, Eusebius notes the corruption of the virginal church introduced by Simon:

> ... from whom came the Simonians, and Cleobius, from whom came the Cleobians, and Dositheus, from whom came the Dositheans, and Gorthæus, from whom came the Goratheni, and Masbotheus, from whom came the Masbothæans. From them sprang the Menandrianists, and Marcionists, and Carpocratians, and Valentinians, and Basilidians, and Saturnilians. Each introduced privately and separately his own peculiar opinion. From them came false Christs, false prophets, false apostles, who divided the unity of the Church by corrupt doctrines uttered against God and against his Christ. (*Eccl. Hist.* 4.22.5)

J. B. Lightfoot's discussion of Ignatius' opponents supports this patristic hypothesis. Ignatius condemns both docetic heretics and Judaizing ones, and does so in a way that indicates that Ignatius viewed them as two sides of the same error. To the Magnesians, for instance, he warns against "heterodoxies and antiquated fables" and says that "if to the present hour we live in the observance of Judaic rites, we confess that we have not received grace." Lightfoot hears echoes of 1 Timothy 1:4, 4:7, and Titus 1:14 here, and concludes that "a closely allied form of Gnostic Judaism is suggested, which taught by myths or fables... the genealogy of angelic beings or emanations, which were intended to bridge over the chasm between God and the World." In his letter to the Philadelphians, Ignatius first denounces Judaism, and then turns to stress the flesh of Jesus, his cross and passion, a sign that the heretics he opposes were denying these things. Lightfoot again finds evidence that

---

16. From the *Apostolic Constitution* (Book 4), Section 7, "Whence the Heresies Sprang, and Who Was the Ringleader of Their Impiety," at http://www.newadvent.org/fathers/07156.htm, accessed August 5, 2009.

"their Judaism was Docetic or Gnostic."[17] In general, Lightfoot concludes that Ignatius' letters "illustrate the truth, which is sufficiently confirmed from other quarters, that the earliest forms of Christian Gnosticism were Judaic." He sees the cross as a particular stumbling block that would trip Jews over into Docetism: "This Docetic view of Christ's humanity would appeal to popular Judaism — the Judaism of the Scribes and Pharisees — only so far as it related to the passion. A suffering Christ was a stumbling-block in the way of popular Messianic conceptions."[18]

More directly relevant to our purposes, 1 John has sometimes been interpreted as a polemic against a Cerinthian heresy.[19] This rests partly on patristic stories about John's near-encounter with Cerinthus at a bathhouse, and it has been used to support the view that John's opponents are proto-Gnostics who teach a semidocetic Christology. But patristic critics not only accuse Cerinthus of gnostic teaching but sometimes condemn him as a Judaizing heretic. A third-century text attached to Tertullian's *Prescription Against Heretics* (the author is known as Pseudo-Tertullian) says (in Raymond Brown's summary) that "Cerinthus taught that the world was created by angels (instead of by a demiurge) who also was responsible for the giving of the law. Pseudo-Tertullian also reports that the Ebionites (a Jewish Christian movement) were the successors of Cerinthus in some of their ideas."[20] The text itself reads:

> After [Carpocrates] broke out the heretic Cerinthus, teaching similarly. For he, too, says that the world was originated by those *angels*; and sets forth Christ as born of the seed of Joseph, contending that He was merely human, without divinity; affirming also that the Law was given by angels; representing the God of the Jews as not the Lord, but an angel. His successor was Ebion,

---

17. Lightfoot, *The Apostolic Fathers* (5 vols.; Peabody, MA: Hendrickson, 1989), Part II, vol. 1, 373–82.

18. *Apostolic Fathers*, Part II, vol. 1, 378–79.

19. The following comes from Raymond Brown, *The Epistles of John* (Anchor Bible; Garden City, NY: Doubleday, 1982), 49–68; Appendix II.

20. Brown, *Epistles*, 768.

not agreeing with Cerinthus in every point; in that he affirms the world to have been made by God, not by angels; and because it is written, "No disciple above *his* master, nor servant above *his* lord," sets forth likewise the law *as binding*, of course for the purpose of excluding the gospel and vindicating Judaism.[21]

In his treatise *Against Heresies* (10.17), Hippolytus also claims that Cerinthus distinguished between God and the demiurgic angelic power who made the world. Dionysius Bar Salibi (d. 1171), basing his opinion on lost works of Hippolytus, also presented Cerinthus as a Jewish figure. Brown writes,

> Dionysius tells us that Gaius (or Caius), a learned ecclesiastic of Rome at the end of the second century . . . , is supposed to have denied that John wrote either Revelation or John, works really composed by Cerinthus. Hippolytus, we are told, disproved this claim of Gaius on the principle that the doctrine of Cerinthus was quite unlike that of John, e.g., Cerinthus taught the necessity of circumcision, that the creator was an angel, that Jesus was not born of a virgin, and that eating and drinking certain things were forbidden.[22]

Epiphanius of Salamis's Panarion (375) records similar details of Cerinthus' teaching. Linking him with the Nazoraeans, a Jewish sect, as well as the Ebionites, he says that Cerinthus was one of the troublemakers in Acts 15. According to Epiphanius, Cerinthus was "the founder of a Jewish Christian sect that remained faithful to circumcision and other observances of the Law; for them Jesus was the Messiah but human and not to be worshipped."[23] This is taken from the *Adanacephalaeosis*, and the whole text is a litany of Jewish-inspired heresies:

---

21. Available online at http://www.newadvent.org/fathers/0319.htm chapter 3 accessed September 23, 2009.
22. Brown, *Epistles*, 768.
23. Brown, *Epistles*, 769.

28. Cerinthians, also known as Merinthians. These are a type of Jew derived from Cerinthus and Merinthus, who boast of circumcision, but say that the world was made by angels and that Jesus was named Christ as an advancement to a higher rank.

29. Nazoraeans, who confess that Christ Jesus is Son of God, but all of whose customs are in accordance with the Law.

30, 1. Ebionites are very like the Cerinthians and Nazoraeans; the sect of the Sampsaeans and Elkasaites was associated with them to a degree.

30, 2. They say that Christ has been created in heaven, also the Holy Spirit. But Christ lodged in Adam at first, and from time to time takes Adam himself off and puts him back on—for this is what they say he did during his visit in the flesh.

30, 3. Although they are Jews they have Gospels, abhor the eating of flesh, take water for God, and, as I said, hold that Christ clothed himself with a man when he became incarnate. They continually immerse themselves in water, summer and winter, if you please for purification like the Samaritans.

Brown evaluates this mixed evidence—Cerinthus was a Gnostic (Irenaeus) and Cerinthus was a Judaizer—and concludes that the former is more reliable. Perhaps, though, it is a mistake to set these off against each other. Perhaps it is better to take both testimonies with equal weight. If John is responding to Cerinthus or his disciples, it may well be he is responding to a complex of Jewish and Gnostic error.

Third, Gnostic texts themselves make it abundantly clear that, even if Judaism is not the sole source of Gnosticism, there are Jewish sources. The *Nag Hammadi* library, discovered in 1945, includes not only overtly Christian texts like the *Gospel of Thomas* and *The Act of Peter*, but also meditations on Jewish figures like Adam, Seth, Shem, and Melchizedek. The figure of Wisdom (Sophia) who often appears in Gnostic texts is arguably of Jewish origin, her fall comparable to the fall of Eve.[24] Some of the texts concerned with Jewish personages also include overtly Christian themes, but not all do. Arising from the "Sethite" sect, the *Apocalypse of Adam* has no overt Christian references, but records a revelation of three visitors to Adam, mediated to Adam by his son Seth. Seth recounts how Adam and Eve lost knowledge by their fall, and how the knowledge communicated to Seth would be preserved until the "Illuminator" arrives.[25]

Even in this text, however, Christian overtones are discernible. According to Seth,

> [o]nce again, for the third time, the illuminator of knowledge will pass by in great glory, in order to leave (something) of the seed of Noah and the sons of Ham and Japheth—to leave for himself fruit-bearing trees. And he will redeem the souls from the day of death. For the whole creation that came from the dead earth will be under the authority of death. But those who reflect upon the knowledge of the eternal God in their heart(s) will not perish. For they have not received spirit from this kingdom alone, but they have received it from an . . . eternal angel. . . . illuminator . . . [will] come upon . . . [that is] dead . . . of Seth. And he will perform signs and wonders in order to score the powers and their ruler.[26]

The fragmentary nature of the last section of the text makes it impossible to be sure, but an illuminator who restores saving knowledge by performing signs and wonders could well be a description of Jesus.

This only scratches the surface of the evidence, but these texts bring to the forefront a set of issues that warrant further study: Was

---

24. George W. MacRae, "The Jewish Background of the Gnostic Sophia Myth," *Novum Testamentum* 12 (1970), 86–101.

25. The text is found in James M. Robinson, ed., *The Nag Hammadi Library* (rev. ed.; San Francisco: Harper & Row, 1988), 279–86.

26. *Nag Hammadi*, 282.

Judaism the main source of Gnosticism, or only *one* minor source? How strong is the evidence for *pre*-Christian Gnosticism within Judaism? If Judaism is a major source for Gnosticism, how do we account for the presence of Christian elements in so many Gnostic texts? What do we make of Edwin Yamauchi's pungent argument that claims about pre-Christian Gnosticism are conjectural, and that the evidence collapses into "a mass of debris"? There is evidence for Jewish influence in Gnosticism, but there is evidence too that Gnosticism arose from Christian sources. Is there a way to make room for both of these lines of evidence?

As noted above, Gnosticism seems polar opposite to Judaism, especially in views of the goodness of the material world, but there are Jewish elements in Gnosticism, and this forces the question: what made certain Jews turn in a Gnostic direction? Perhaps this turn comes from syncretic contact with Hellenistic or Iranian styles of thought. Perhaps, though, the reaction arises from Jewish revulsion against incarnation. Saying creation is good is one thing; saying that God assumes a created nature is quite another, and incarnation might be especially offensive for Jews who believe Jesus' basic claim to be Messiah. Thus, Judaism per se is not the source of Gnosticism; rather, Gnosticism arises from a Judaism that has become Christian, only to revert back to Judaism. The Jewish source of Gnosticism is a Judaism touched both by Christianity and by anti-Christian animus.

Is there evidence that John is writing to warn his churches about the dangers of Judaizing Gnosticism, or gnosticizing Judaism? I think so.

CLINGING TO DARKNESS

Jews are clearly Jesus' main opponents in the gospels, and throughout Acts the apostles suffer persecution exclusively from Jewish enemies. Though John's gospel has long been viewed by scholars and laymen as a "spiritual gospel," a Hellenistic gospel with some unclear relation to early Gnosticism, it is fully engaged with Jewish concerns. It is true that some of the best known and most precious "spiritual" passages of the New Testament come from John's gospel, but so do some of the sharpest denunciations of Jews.

Page through John's gospel, especially chapters 5 through 10, and see how the bulk of the material is made up of contentious, endless, and unresolved conflicts, arguments, and debates between Jesus and the Jews. Some of these conflicts take on the flavor of a legal process, with people being interrogated, witnesses being called, a judge and jury set up. Jesus is on trial throughout the gospel.[27]

Specifically, he is on trial before the "Jews," a term that is used in several different ways in the gospel. At times, the word is used in a neutral sense, as when John refers to the "feasts of the Jews." Sometimes, "Jew" refers simply to those who live in Judea, and those who practice the worship and life of the Old Covenant (12:9–12). Most of the time, the word has a negative connotation, and Brown suggests that it is "almost a technical title for the religious authorities, particularly those in Jerusalem, who are hostile to Jesus" (cf. 8:13, 18ff.; 9:22; 18:3, 12).

John gives us a symbolic hint of this central conflict at the beginning of his gospel. John begins with references to the creation account (John 1:1; Gen. 1:1), not only using the phrase "in the beginning" but also referring to the radiance of light on Day 1 of creation (John 1:4–5; Gen. 1:3–5). Dark and light are often seen as moral terms (dark = evil, light = good), but in the original creation account, darkness is not evil since there is no evil. Rather, darkness is simply prior to the light. Creation is originally dark, formless, empty. As Yahweh goes about the task of illuminating, forming, and filling, he first creates light, which he judges "good" (Gen. 1:4). He separates light and darkness, but this separation is nowhere explicitly designated as "good," as, for instance, the separation of waters on the third day is "good" (1:10). In a general sense, since the creation as a whole is "good" (1:31), the alternation of light and

27. On this, see Andrew Lincoln, *Truth on Trial: The Lawsuit Motif in the Fourth Gospel* (Hendrickson, 2000).

darkness must be good as well. However, darkness is never designated as such, nor is the alternation of light and dark explicitly described as good. The reason has to do with eschatology: just as the second day's separation of waters above and below is not called good because it is not permanent, so the separation of light and darkness is not good because it will one day yield to permanent, uninterrupted light (Rev. 22:5). Our world of alternating light and darkness is good, but it is not the final goodness of the completed creation. In Genesis, in short, darkness is the time before light; it is not bad, but it is not fully good. It is not bad, merely early. Darkness is protological; light, eschatological.

In John, the fundamental dualism of light and darkness is the same as in Genesis, not moral but temporal and eschatological. For John as for Genesis, dark is the period of day before dawn; light is daytime. Darkness is thus the symbol of the Old Covenant, while light is symbol of the New. Darkness is part of the "good" creation, and is good to that extent; but it is so only because the darkness gives way to the light. Similarly, when history is looked at as a whole, the darkness of the Old Covenant is "good," but it is so only because it prepares for the coming sunrise.

This makes good sense of John's first use of light and dark in his gospel (1:4–5). He alludes to the creation account ("in the beginning," 1:1), where darkness is not "evil" but simply precedes light. The Word, which is the light of men, shines into the darkness and the darkness can neither "overcome" nor "comprehend" it (John uses a characteristic double entendre). We know that the Word/light is Jesus, and as the gospel proceeds it becomes clear that the opponents of light are the Jews who resist Jesus. They are the "darkness" into which the light shines, the darkness that attempts to overcome the light but cannot. Their fundamental sin is to cling to night after day has come, thinking they can be disciples of Moses without honoring Jesus (cf. 9:28–29). When John says that men love darkness rather than light because their deeds are evil (3:19), he is saying that they love the evening of the Old Covenant rather than the daylight of the New Covenant because the old system provided a protective covering for sin.

23

John uses the imagery in the same way in his letters. This is most obvious in 1 John 2:8–11. Verse 8 claims that the darkness is passing away. If "darkness" means "evil," John's statement is flatly false: two thousand years later, after Stalin and Hitler and Mao and Pol Pot, evil has *not* passed away. "Darkness" must be something that is giving way to light *in John's own time*. If we take "darkness" to refer to the preparatory stage for the coming of God's Light, it makes sense: the true light, Jesus, is already shining, and because of that the darkness of the old system is passing away, though not yet completely gone. John writes at a time when the last hour of night is passing, and day is about to begin.

This has important implications for how John views the relation of Old and New. According to John (and the other writers of the New Testament), the New Covenant is not a softer, gentler covenant, a covenant that lowers the requirements and gives sinners a paternal pat on the head. The New is preeminently a covenant of judgment. Light comes and suddenly everyone can see, and in the Bible seeing means judging. Light comes, and humanity suddenly finds itself exposed to the searching gaze of the Judge of all the earth. The coming of the light does not cover sin but exposes it. During the Old Covenant, God winked at sin, but now the times of ignorance come to an end (Acts 17:30), and God calls all men everywhere to repent or face judgment. The Hebrew word for atonement, *kipper*, basically means "cover," and this is what the rites and institutions of the Old Covenant did: they screened people from full exposure to the light, so that Israel in her flesh and pollution could endure living in God's presence. Yahweh himself is enthroned in light and glory, but in the Old Covenant he was enthroned behind a veil. With the coming of the New Covenant, Yahweh steps through the veil of the firmament to meet us in our own flesh, to shine the light in our faces, and then rends the veil in the death and resurrection of Jesus to fill the earth with the glory of his righteousness.

CONCLUSION

Judaizing is just this: converted Jews want to remain in the darkness of the old system, hoping to synthesize darkness and light and thinking they can cover over their sins through performance of temple rites and sacrifices. Exposed to the light of day, the light of full manhood, they want to crawl back into the womb, but they can't. Light has come, the living Word sharper than a sword, and now all stands bare before the eyes of him with whom we have to do. If you're a Judaizer, you don't want to hear about incarnation; you don't want to know that God has pitched his tent in human flesh. You want to deny that Jesus is the Christ, and that Christ has come in the flesh. You want the comfort and safety of shadows.

This is Judaizing, and Gnosticism arises from the same set of fears and desires. Under the old order, God acted through mediating beings. Angels delivered the law (Gal. 3:19), and when Yahweh appeared in the Old Testament, he appeared as an Angel. Judaizing is a denial of historical progress, an arrested adolescence that refuses to die to childhood and accept adulthood. Judaizers of the first century wanted to stay in the world of mediating angels; they didn't want to grow into the awesome reality that God had come to humanity as a man. That is Gnosticism as well, the desire to remain at a safe distance from God, the desire to have contact only with God's menial messengers.

During the period of the Old Covenant, further, God hid things. He hid some things inside the Most Holy Place, where no one could go, and he hid his plans from his people (which is why Paul calls the gospel a "mystery"). He had a secret, which was disclosed, and then only in part, to certain *cognoscenti*—priests and prophets. The gospel opens the veil, makes secrets known, brings an end to taboo by revealing the mystery. In Christ, we know what God's plan is; the living Word, the eternal Decree and Will of the Father, has become flesh and dwelt and spoken and acted among us. The apostles touched and saw him, *touched* the *Holy One* of Israel. In this age, God opens his purposes to us without veiling, without secrets. All that was whispered is proclaimed from the housetops; all that was in shadows is brought to the light. Judaizing attempts to maintain the age of secrecy that Jesus brought to an end; so does Gnosticism.

Above all, in the Old Covenant, Yahweh hid himself, in a cloud, behind the billowing cloudlike veils of the tabernacle, behind the oil wood doors of the Most Holy Place. But he hides no longer. Judaizers do not believe that, and neither do Gnostics. Judaizing is a theology of an intact veil,[28] and so is Gnosticism. Both deny the rapturous declaration of the opening verses of 1 John, that God emerged from the twilight and shone like the Sun in visible, audible, tangible flesh.

---

28. See the sad and brilliant article by David Gelernter, "Judaism Beyond Words: Part II," *Commentary* (September 2002), which argues that the intact veil separating God and man is not a temporary reality but a key symbol, part of the genius of Judaism.

2

STRUCTURE

The structure of 1 John has been analyzed inconclusively for a long time,[1] and I don't pretend to bring that discussion to an end with the few comments that follow. Instead, I offer what I hope are illuminating structural observations, and leave the more detailed discussions to the remainder of the commentary.

First, since the earliest centuries of the church, commentators have noted the similarities between the language of the gospel of John and his epistles. I suggest we go further and seek a common structural principle between the two books. John opens his gospel with the declaration about the Word who was with God and was God from the beginning, the Word in whom is life and light

---

1. See the proposal of John Christopher Thomas, "The Literary Structure of 1 John," *Novum Testamentum* 40:4 (1998), 369–81. Thomas refers to the helpful chart of Raymond Brown in *The Epistles of John* (Garden City, NY: Doubleday, 1982), 764.

(John 1:1–5). John begins his epistle with a cluster of the same words: beginning, Word, life, light (1 John 1:1–5). Though not every parallel between the two documents fits into a structural sequence, the letter roughly follows the order of the gospel:

1 John	John
Light in darkness, 1:5–6; 2:9–10	Jesus' conversation with Nicodemus, ch. 3
Denying that Jesus is the Christ, 2:22	Opposition of Jews, chs. 5–9
Sinners of the devil; murderers, 3:1–8, 15	Liars and murderers like the devil, 8:44
Destroy works of devil, 3:8	Prince of this world cast out, 12:30–32
Command to love one another, 3:23	Commandment to love, 13:34; 15:12
Promise of the Spirit, 3:24–4:6	Promise of the Spirit, 14:17; 15:26; 16:13
Mutual abiding, 4:13, 15	Mutual abiding, chs. 15, 17
Overcoming the world, 5:4	Overcoming the world, 16:33
Water and blood, 5:6–8	Water and blood at the cross, 19:34
Written that you may believe, 5:13	Written that you may believe, 20:30–31

1 John, in short, moves from a prologue, to an exhortation to walk in light as Jesus did, to a warning about the worldly opposition that the readers will experience, to a description of the diabolical source of that opposition and a promise that Jesus triumphs over the devil, to a promise of the Spirit and a command to love, and ends with a reference to the crucifixion of the Christ. John's gospel moves from a prologue, through an account of Jesus' early ministry and his "walk," to an account of the intensifying opposition from the Jews, to a heated exchange where Jesus accuses the Jews of following the lead of their father the devil, to Jesus' decla-

ration of his power to overcome Satan, to the Upper Room where he discourses on the Spirit and love, to the cross where Jesus sheds his blood and gives over the water of the Spirit.

According to Warren Gage and Fowler White, John and Revelation are parallel chiasms, centering respectively on John 12 and Revelation 12. The two central passages deal with Jesus' triumph over Satan: John 12 includes Jesus' declaration that the prince of this world is cast out, and Revelation 12 is the vision of the dragon being toppled from his position in heaven. 1 John centers on a similar theme, the assurance that "the Son of God appeared for this purpose, that he might destroy the works of the devil" (3:8).

I have suggested that the letter "centers" on this section, and I need to justify that claim. For starters, a quick assessment of the letter suggests that the middle of chapter 3 is roughly the middle of the book. More elaborately, the letter as a whole can be divided into seven large sections.[2] The first section is 1:1–2:17, and the structure of that section is complex. In the commentary, I divide the first section into three units, each of which has a structural integrity of its own. Yet, the whole forms a unit framed by a number of parallel themes and words: "beginning" (1:1; 2:13, 14); "eyes" (1:1; 2:11, 16; these are the only times *opthalmon* appears in the letter); "word" (1:1; 2:14);[3] "eternal" (*aiōnion* in 1:2 and *aiōn* in 2:17). Yet, in the end, it seems best to regard 1:1–4 as a separate "prologue" to the whole, since John announces his purpose for writing in 1:5 with a formal opening: "this is the message we have heard from Him and announce to you," and because John begins in 1:5 to introduce the light/dark imagery that carries him into chapter 2. As I explain below, 2:18–29 forms a coherent unit, but verses 28 and 29 also function as the opening to the following unit that runs to the end of chapter 3, and this forms the fourth section, 2:28–3:24. Verses 4:1–6

---

2. I found many of Thomas's suggestions helpful, but he does not explain the subdivisions of the text, and some of his divisions divide sections that are structurally united.

3. After 2:14, *logon* does not appear again until 3:18.

form the fifth, 4:7–5:5 form the sixth, and 5:6–21 form the closing section of the letter.

These sections are arranged into a fairly neat heptamerous (seven-part) chiasm:

A. Concerning the word of life, 1:1–4
 B. Walking in light and love, 1:5–2:17
  C. Antichrists and the anointing, 2:18–29
   D. Loving the brethren; Jesus destroyed the devil, 2:28–3:24
  C′ Antichrists and the Spirit, 4:1–6
 B′ God is Love, 4:7–5:5
A′ Spirit, Water, Blood, 5:6–21

The fact that there are seven sections to the letter suggests links with the days of creation:

1 John	Genesis 1
Word and light, 1:1–5	Day 1: Light, separation of light/dark
Jesus as propitiation, 2:2	Day 2: Insertion of firmament
Christ vs. Antichrist	Day 3: Separation of water and land
Jesus overthrows the devil, 3:8	Day 4: Rulers in the heavens
Conflict of spirits, 4:1–6	Day 5: Birds and fish
Community of love, 4:7–5:5	Day 6: Creation of Adam and Eve
The Son of God coming, 5:6, 20	Day 7: Sabbath and parousia of Yahweh

Not all of these fit well (Day 5 doesn't seem to fit at all), but a sufficient number do fit to suggest that there is something to the comparison.

This simple overview does not begin to capture the intricate spirals of John's style, and most of the chapters of the commentary include additional, more detailed structural analysis. The outline above is sufficient to orient the reader to the movement of the book, and indicates that John's exhortation to love the brethren, and his announcement that Jesus has come to destroy Satan's works, stand at the center of the letter.

3

THE WORD OF LIFE
1 John 1:1–4

^{1 John 1:1}That which was from the beginning, which we have heard, which we have seen with our eyes, which we looked upon and have touched with our hands, concerning the word of life—²the life was made manifest, and we have seen it, and testify to it and proclaim to you the eternal life, which was with the Father and was made manifest to us—³that which we have seen and heard we proclaim also to you, so that you too may have fellowship with us; and indeed our fellowship is with the Father and with his Son Jesus Christ. ⁴And we are writing these things so that our joy may be complete.

John writes to a church in crisis. Some are "walking in darkness," hostile to Christian brothers: "The one who loves his brother abides in the light and there is no cause of stumbling in him. But the one who hates his brother is in the darkness and walks in the darkness, and does not know where he is going because the darkness has blinded his eyes" (2:10–11). In John's churches, brothers war with one another, hating rather than loving each other.

Worse, some have turned to the devil: "By this the children of God and the children of the devil are obvious: anyone who does not practice righteousness is not of God, nor the one who does not love his brother. For this is the message which you heard from the beginning, that we should love one another; not as Cain, who was of the evil one, and slew his brother. And for what reason did he slay him? Because his deeds were evil and his brother's were righteous" (3:10–12).

Others have gone out as if they were commissioned by the apostles, though they never really were with the apostles: "They went out from us, but they were not of us; for if they had been of use, they would have remained with us; but they went out in order that it might be shown that they all are not of us" (2:19).[1]

False teachers threaten those who remain and seduce them from Jesus. They deny Jesus as the Messiah, associating with a movement John calls "antichrist." False prophets mislead the church, and John writes to deliver his flock from predators: "These things I have written to you concerning those who are trying to deceive you" (2:26). As Jesus had predicted, the disciples suffer the same assaults as Jesus himself did (John 15–16). The world hated Jesus, and the world hates the disciples of Jesus. There was a traitor among the Twelve, and there are traitors among the churches. Jesus witnessed faithfully in the face of murderous pressure, and his disciples are called to the same courageous faith.

How does John deal with these divisions, conflicts, and threats? In the opening verses, he emphasizes the fellowship that believers have with one another and with the apostles. His message is that his readers should walk in light rather than darkness, and walking in light means walking in love. He commits his message to writing so that there will be joy among both the apostles and the

---

1. The precise force of 2:19 is disputed, and we will examine it more carefully in chapter 6 below.

readers of his letter. In short, he exhorts his readers to love and unity.

Yet this is not where he begins. He begins by pointing back to the fundamental evangelical announcement: God the Word, the Life, has come near. When he sees the churches falling apart, John addresses the problem by first talking about the incarnation.

Woodenly translated, verses 1–4 say:

> What was from the beginning, what we have heard, what we have seen with our eyes, what we have gazed upon and our hands handled concerning the word of life—and the life was manifested, and we have seen and bear witness and announce to you the life, the eternal one, which was toward the Father and was manifested to us—what we have seen and heard, we announce also to you. . . .

The text gives an impression of breathless starts and stops, the words of a man in possession of some towering cosmic truth, who cannot wait to get it out but who is too excited to finish his sentence before moving on to the next thought. Despite this appearance, the opening verses are tightly structured:[2]

A. What was from the beginning
  B. what we have heard
    C. what we have seen with our eyes
      D. what we have gazed upon and our
         hands have handled
        E. concerning the Word of Life
      D' life was manifested
    C' what we have seen
  B' and heard
A' we announce also to you.

The second D section is the most complicated part of the passage, but it too is a small chiasm:

---

2. Thanks to James Jordan for suggesting this structural analysis.

A. Life was manifested and *we* have seen
  B. and we bear witness and announce to *you*
A' the Life, the Eternal, which was manifested to *us*.

D' expands on the central section, which introduces the Word of Life, and also anticipates the end of the passage, the announcement of the manifestation of the Word to the readers. D' is a microcosm of the whole passage, moving from what "we" have seen to what is announced to "you."

John not only begins with theology, but with controversial theology. One of the debates wracking the churches concerns the incarnation of the Word, and John begins by declaring that the Word has become visible, audible, tangible. Instead of trying to find some common ground, a milquetoast confession that would be satisfactory to troublers of the church, John immediately gives a divisive confession of faith in Jesus the Word of Life.

Massaging the message may seem wise to us, but that is the wisdom of the world. John knows that God brings unity through division. To reunite a divided world, he brings not peace but a sword. When the nations were scattered at Babel, he called Abraham and cut his seed off from the nations, a deeper wound in humanity than even the divisions of Babel, a wound healed only by a cross and resurrection. When there were tensions in Israel between North and South, Yahweh split the nation in two, and then he divided the Northern kingdom in two again by sending Elijah and Elisha. He formed a people in which there is no slave nor free, no male or female, no Jew nor Greek by sending Jesus, who was opposed and hated and the source of turmoil and strife within Israel. From the beginning of the world, from the first week of creation, God formed a unified world by first dividing it. The world of light comes long after Yahweh divides light from darkness, heaven and earth are reunited only after being separated by a firmament veil, and the knowledge of the Lord will cover the earth as the waters cover the sea long after Yahweh has separated water from water so dry land can emerge.

We moderns think unity is easy. We only have to sit down and talk and everyone will rise from the conference table filled with the glow of love and peace. The Bible knows that this is a delusion. Unity is costly, achieved only by the anguish of crucifixion. Unity seems easy for us only because of the bloody cross of Jesus, and the blood of many martyrs since.

As a witness to the Word of creation, John divides—just like the double-edged Word itself. John wants the church unified in brotherly love, but he knows that there is only one means for the church to be unified. Unity in the human race can be achieved only if the human race is united with the unity in the Spirit that exists between the Father and Son, and that is only possible because of the reality of incarnation. The church is *not* united by common ideas. It is united as a people, in flesh and blood, the flesh and blood assumed by the Son. If the incarnation is the basis for Christian unity, it makes no sense to say that we can be unified and yet *deny* the incarnation. The church is not unified because we believe the incarnation. We are unified because the incarnation is real. But if we do not believe it, the unity it achieves does not realize itself in our lives together. Where the incarnation is denied, the church cannot *be* and certainly cannot be *one*.

To address divisions and threats of the church, John begins with a confession about Jesus, a confession of realities that are essential to the unity and health of the new humanity of the church. It is a complex confession.

BEGINNINGS

First, it's a confession about beginnings.

Is John talking about the beginning of all things, the beginning of all beginnings? Not necessarily. At times, he and the other apostles are witnesses of what has happened "from the beginning" (cf. Acts 1:22; 1 John 2:24; 3:11), and that beginning is the beginning of the ministry of John or Jesus. Possibly, John opens his first letter talking about the beginning of the gospel story. On the other hand, John begins his gospel with the phrase "in the beginning," and there the phrase does refer to the beginning of all things. Elsewhere in 1 John, he uses "beginning" to refer to things at the very beginning. He writes to fathers, he says in 2:13–14, because they know the "one who has been from the beginning." In chapter 3, he points to the devil who has "sinned from the beginning," clearly a reference to the serpent's temptation in Genesis 3.[3]

Commentators are divided on which direction to go here, but given John's penchant for puns and double entendres, it is likely that the word points in several directions at once. Especially in John, the word "beginning" (archē) cannot help but conjure Genesis 1:1, and this connection is reinforced by other allusions to Genesis 1: the "Word of Life" is the word by which God spoke creation into being (1 John 1:1); the contrast of light and darkness recalls the work of the first day (Gen. 1:1–5; cf. John 1:4–5, 9); as we shall see, the word for "propitiation" (Greek, hilasmon) is connected with the "firmament" that divided the waters above from the waters below (1 John 2:2; cf. Gen. 1:6–8). Yet, the specific beginning he announces is the beginning that occurred when the Word of Life appeared. When we think about the appearance of the Word, however, John wants us to think simultaneously about the beginning of all things. By alluding to the "beginning" of Genesis 1, he wants to emphasize that the incarnation of the Word is the beginning of a new beginning. It's the beginning of a new creation story.

"Incarnation" here does not simply refer to the fact that the eternal Word became flesh and blood but to the entire life and ministry of Jesus. That is the point of the odd grammar of the first lines of the letter, where John uses a neuter pronoun (translated "that which" or "what") even though its antecedent, "Word" (Greek, logos), is masculine. This encompasses not just Jesus the person but his work.[4] The appearance of the Word in tangible human flesh, his life of ministry within Israel, his death on the cross and his resurrection—all this constitutes the new beginning of the world.

---

3. Overall, John uses the word "beginning" (archē) nine times in his first letter.
4. Stott, Letters, loc. cit.

LIFE

Second, it is a confession about the source of life.

Jesus is described here as the "Word of Life" and as "the eternal life" (vv. 1–2). He does not simply *have* life, nor is he a lifeless conduit of life. He *is* life, and he is life because the Father has given him to have life in himself, to have the life of the Spirit in full measure (John 5:26). We might be misled by centuries of Christian pietism to think that the life John announces is an internal spiritual reality, or disembodied life in heaven. But life means life. God has all abundance, energy, joy, delight, buoyancy in himself and he has communicated this abundant life to his Word. He has chosen not to keep all this eternal and infinite liveliness to himself. From the beginning, in all eternity, this life was something shared. As Stott points out, the Son did not exist from eternity in a state of splendid isolation. The life that existed prior to the manifestation of life was already life *shared* by the Father and the Son. According to John's gospel, the Life that is the Word was "toward" the Father from all eternity (1:1). In the incarnation, God turned himself inside out, so that the Word of Life is toward us. That means that life in all its teeming energy is offered to us.

John's reference to "what our hands handled" (v. 1) refers specifically to the disciples' touching of Jesus after his resurrection (Luke 24:39; John 20:27). Jesus is the Word of Life, the eternal life, supremely in his resurrection from the dead. Handling the Word of Life that created all things is a fairly astonishing experience in any age, but it would have had particular import for the apostles. "Do not touch" is the recurrent prohibition not only in ancient Israel but in ancient paganism. Ancient religion—and tribal religions still today, like Islam—centered on things taboo, things untouchable because of their earthiness and impurity or because of their transcendent holiness. Religion for the ancients was about *not* walking *here*, *not* touching *that*, *not* looking at *that*. Jew and Gentile, all were under guardians and managers, no better than slaves and small children (Gal. 4:1–7). Along comes John, announcing that the most transcendent reality of all—the Life, the eternal Life, the one from the beginning—this reality has become visible, audible, tangible. Human hands have touched life-become-human-flesh.

Seeing the Word is equally novel. Verbs for "seeing" are used four times in these opening verses. Though "touching" is the climax of the sequence of verbs, sight receives emphasis. Seeing the Word is what makes the apostles into witnesses. It was an axiom, as John himself puts it at the beginning of his gospel, that "no man has seen God at any time." Yet along comes John, announcing that the invisible God has made himself visible in his Word. Moses could not look at the face of God, but saw only the back side. Israel could not gaze at the glory of God as it was revealed on Sinai and in the tabernacle. No one entered the Most Holy Place to gaze at the glory of God, since Yahweh had, for Israel's own protections, shrouded himself in tent curtains and behind doors. According to John, the apostles have seen the God who was veiled and covered in layers of cloud, and they have been able to look him in the face.

By the mere fact of incarnation, God brought an end to the ancient system of religion, in Israel and elsewhere. By coming out from behind the curtains, he annuled all the holiness codes of antiquity.

Because John and the apostles ("we") see, hear, touch, they become "angels," messengers and witnesses who proclaim (*apagellomen*) eternal life (v. 2). In this function as "witnesses"[5] who then "proclaim," the apostles fulfill the role assigned to Israel in the great contest between Yahweh and the nations. Scripturally, witnesses testify on behalf of Yahweh, proclaiming before the nations his righteousness and faithfulness.[6] John and the other apostles are

---

5. The word for "witness" or "testify" is *martureō*, from which the English "martyr" is derived. The Greek verb is used six times in 1 John (1:2; 4:14; 5:6, 7, 9, 10), and the noun form is used another six times (5:9–11), for a total of twelve. John has constructed the letter to suggest a twelve-fold witness, the witness of the true Israel.

6. The *Theological Dictionary of the New Testament* article on "witness" summarizes this neatly. "We refer to the sections Is. 43:9–13 and 44:7–11. Here Yahweh arranges before the nations a kind of trial in which it will be shown who is truly God, Yahweh or the gods of the Gentiles. The nations seem to be here both spectators and also judges who will decide (v. Rad). But they are also interested parties as advocates and witnesses on behalf of their gods. They are interested witnesses who

witnesses of God's final climactic act of power and deliverance, witnesses to the incarnation of the Word of Life. They take up God's cause when the nations accuse him. When the nations charge that God is inaccessible and uncaring, the apostles bear witness that God has not remained hidden, nor has he left his world in ruins. He has come to bring life. At the same time, they take up God's cause against the nations. Because the light has come into the world, everyone everywhere must now repent and believe. Because light has come, judgment has come, and the hidden God will no longer overlook the sin that has been covered by darkness.

From John's emphasis on the visibility and tangibility of the Word, Eastern Orthodox Christians have concluded that we are no longer forbidden, as Israel was, to communicate with God through images. Under the Old Covenant, images were prohibited because God had not shown himself. Now that he has shown himself, images are permissible, not only as adornments but for veneration.

This is not, however, the direction John goes. He emphasizes that the apostles have seen and gazed "with their eyes" on the Word made flesh. After these opening verses, however, John virtually drops the theme of sight. The verb "see" (*oraō*) occurs a significant seven times in the letter, but the word is most concentrated at the beginning (1:1, 2, 3; 3:2, 6; 4:20 [twice]). Elsewhere, John refers to "eyes" only twice more, both negatively (2:11, 16). The verb "behold" (*theaomai*) occurs again only in 4:12 and 14. Oddly, though, 4:12 seems directly to contradict the excited declaration of the prologue: "God no one at any time has beheld." And

---

must come forward to demonstrate the deity of their gods from their experiences (43:9; 44:9). To this extent they are also accusers of Yahweh, though vanquished by Him, 44:11. For these witnesses or deities have nothing whereof to testify. They see nothing and hear nothing. The makers of idols are impotent. Their favoured gods are of no use to them. In this trial they will be put to shame (44:9–11). In contrast, Israel is told three times: 'You are my witnesses,' 43:10, 12; 44:8. . . . In this trial between God and the nations and their gods, Israel, on the basis of the guidance, deliverance and revelation which is grounded in its election and which it has experienced, will declare to the nations of the world the uniqueness, reality, and deity of God. Hence they are His witnesses."

4:20 reiterates the point: "whoever does not love his brother whom he has seen, the *God whom he has not seen* he is not able to love."

What is John saying? He announces that the Word of Life has become visible, and that he is an eyewitness of the Son, but then toward the end of the letter, he is still saying that "no one has seen God." What gives? The answer, in part, is a trinitarian answer (aren't *all* answers trinitarian?). The *Father* has not been seen; he has never appeared in his person, but has shown himself in his Son, so that whoever sees the Son has seen the Father (John 14:9). The opening verses of the letter announce that God has emerged from hiding, becoming visible, audible, tangible in the Incarnate Son. Yet, the Father—often the referent of the word "God" in the New Testament—still is not seen, but is known in his Word.

However, this is not the full answer. John's opening verses move from the visibility of the Son to the audibility of the apostles. The verb "see" is used seven times in the letter, but the verb "hear" is used twice as much, fourteen times (1:1, 3, 5; 2:7, 18, 24 [twice]; 3:11; 4:3, 5, 6 [twice]; 5:14, 15). If this were merely a matter of numbers, it would not be very weighty.[7] More weighty is the overall movement of the opening verses of the letter. Life is available to us through the Word of Life, now manifested in human flesh, but there is an order to this manifestation. The apostles had direct access to the visible and tangible Word. We do not. Living twenty centuries from the ascension, we have *not* heard, seen, beheld, or handled him. Instead, we rely on the testimony of the "we." Through fellowship or communion with them, we have fellowship with the Father and the Son (v. 3), and we have communion with them by believing their *written* testimony concerning the Word of Life (v. 4) and by abiding in the community of which they are the foundation stones (cf. Eph. 2:20). John moves from telling us that he and the apostles have seen and touched life to telling us that he announces this discovery to us. If we want to have life, we have to

---

7. The mere fact that one word is used more than another does not, of course, necessarily indicate anything about the content of a text. "And" (*kai*) is used more than either "see" or "hear," but it would be nonsense to say that John's letter is about "andness" or represents an exercise in "andology."

receive the announcement, the gospel proclamation. What they have seen and touched, we access by hearing. John emphasizes as strongly as possible the visibility of the Word, but then falls back to the old Hebraic emphasis on the ear. The movement is from their eyes and hands to our ears. We have not seen the Word, and we do not need to. We have the law, the prophets, and now the apostles. That is more than enough.

TESTIMONY

The one thing that we have left to "see" is the written text of 1 John (v. 4). We cannot see Jesus anymore. We cannot even hear the voices of the apostles. But John has committed his message to writing, and we still have that. We can hear it read, and see the text itself. That is how we come to know the Word that appeared at the beginning to make a new beginning.

Relying on apostolic testimony is troublesome for many Christians. Our knowledge of Jesus seems much less reliable than that of the apostles. Like Thomas, we want to see it for ourselves, to touch the wounds and look Jesus in the eye. This demand is, of course, foolish on the face of it. Much of what we know about anything is based on testimony. Do you know that China exists? Have you seen it? Did Napoleon conquer Europe? Have you ever touched an atom or an electron? Could Osama bin Laden be an elaborate hoax concocted by a paranoid Bush administration with the cooperation of the media?

We rely on testimony every day. Was your wife overcharged at the grocery? Did you see it happen? Did the boss tell a gross joke to your husband at work? Did you hear it? Did your toddler throw a tantrum while the sitter was minding her? How can you be sure the sitter didn't provoke it by sticking needles into your child's toes? We cannot avoid relying on testimony, and the only question is whether the testimony is reliable, whether the witnesses are trustworthy.

We often think fondly of how wonderful it would have been to be alive in Palestine when Jesus was around. We would not have to believe on the testimony of anyone else. We could have seen all those miracles with our own eyes. We would not have to hear about people handling Jesus; we could have touched him with our own hands. We could have sat with him at a meal. But being there was not a guarantee of being a disciple. Many saw the miracles and either denied them, or found some alternative explanation for them, or hated Jesus for stirring the pot. Many people touched Jesus only to lay hands on him to arrest and kill him. Had we been there, we might well have been in the crowd clamoring to lynch him.

More importantly, Jesus told his disciples that it was good for them that he was going away. When I leave, he said, I will send my Spirit to be with you, and because the Spirit will be with you, you will do greater things than I have done (John 14:12). We might think it would be better to have been there then, but in fact it is better for us to be here now. Jesus said so.

Despite appearances, we are even more intimate with Jesus than the disciples were prior to his ascension and Pentecost. They heard him speak, but often misunderstood what he said. Though we also get things wrong, we have the Spirit to lead us into truth. Did the apostles even know that Jesus was the Word made flesh, made tangible? Or was that an insight they came to after the wonder of resurrection? Now we know who he is. They touched him with their hands, but he did not dwell in them through his Spirit; he does now. They could eat with him at his table, but they did not feed on him, so that he became bone of their bone and flesh of their flesh. But we do: we receive his body and blood at his table.

FELLOWSHIP WITH US

This intimacy is what John is getting at when he talks about the communion of the church with apostles, the Father, and Jesus. There is a necessary order here. We have no communion with the Father without communion with the Son; no communion with the Son without communion with the apostles; and no communion with the apostles without receiving their written testimony in the communion of the church. Like the life that existed from the beginning, which was with the Father, the life now manifested and is available to us is a life in communion, a shared life. Scripture knows no life that is not shared life, life *together*. To paraphrase Paul, life comes from communion and communion comes from hearing and hearing from the Word of Life.

This intimacy of communion with God is a blessing of the New Covenant, the new beginning. In the Old Testament, Israel knew of table fellowship between Yahweh and his people, of a marital covenant. Abraham was a "friend of God," and we are all sons of Abraham, but not until Philo is *koinōnia* used openly and repeatedly to describe this relationship with God, and only in the New Testament does this really come into full expression, since only in the New Testament is there something in "common" between God and man: the "common" God-man Jesus, and the "common" Spirit shared by Father and Son. In the incarnation, the Word becomes our *go'el*, our *kinsman* redeemer.

What does it mean to have communion with the Father and with his son, Jesus? In context, John surely means to emphasize that we have a share in the life that was with the Father and manifested to us. Whatever life God has in himself, in the Son, he shares with us. More concretely, Paul describes fellowship with Jesus in terms of fellowship in his whole life—in his life, sufferings, death, resurrection. Believers have communion with one another—sharing life, projects, ministries, tears, wealth, laughter, meals, evenings, cigars. This life-together is joyous and vibrant because it is also an inclusion in and is permeated by the life of the Father and Son in the Spirit, manifested in Jesus.

This common life is a life of joy (v. 4). Manuscripts differ: some say that the letter is written to complete the joy of the apostles ("our joy"), while others say that the letter is written to complete the joy of the readers ("your joy"). Whatever the original reading, the result is the same. The apostles' joy is completed, certainly, when the readers believe the eyewitness, and share in the fellowship they have with Father and Son. If John writes to fulfill the joy of the readers, that certainly implies joy from him. The point is that the joy, like the life, is *shared* joy.

John writes to a divided church, a church in crisis. How is such a church to be unified? Not by common ideas, but by a Person, the Person of the Eternal Life manifested from the Father. The church is unified only by miraculous reality, which it proclaims in a radically divisive confession, the confession that life is available *only* through the Eternal Life that was with God from the beginning, the Eternal Life that has come near as Jesus, to be heard, seen, gazed upon, and handled by the apostles. The church is unified by a radically divisive adherence to the witness of the apostles, committed to writing in the New Testament.

4

WALKING IN LIGHT
1 John 1:5–2:11

The chapter division in our Bibles does not follow the flow of John's argument, which slips past the end of chapter 1 and runs into the beginning of chapter 2. The first verses of chapter 2 deal with sin, the topic in 1:8–10. The word "sin" is first used in the letter at the end of 1:7, and then used another seven times in 1:8–2:2. The noun or verb "sin" occurs another twenty or so times in the letter, but this cluster of eight uses marks this as a distinct unit.

Further, John mentions the light/darkness contrast at the beginning and end of this section (1:5–7; 2:8b–11), again framing these verses as a distinct paragraph. The word "light" is used six times in 1 John, and these references are clustered in 1:5–7 and 2:8–10. "Darkness" is also used six times, and its distribution is virtually the same (twice in 1:5–6, four times in 2:8–11). John's five uses of "walk" are distributed in a similar fashion. Three appear at the beginning and end of this section—twice in 1:6–7, once in 2:11. Thus, along with the light/darkness contrast, "walk" frames this section. The other two uses of "walk" in 1 John are found at the center of this section (2:6), so that the thematic ends of the section meet in the middle.

This section is chiastically arranged:

A. Light and darkness, 1:5–7
  B. Sin and forgiveness, 1:8–2:2
    C. Keeping the commandments, 2:3–5
      D. Walk as he walked, 2:6
    C′ The new commandment, 2:7–8
A′ Light and darkness, 2:9–11

The fact that there is no section on "sin" corresponding to B in the chiasm is intriguing, since all the other sections match so neatly. Perhaps the "hatred for the brethren" in 2:9 and 11 matches "sin" in 1:8–2:2, but the word "sin" is not used after 2:2, and John's treatment of hatred is embedded in a section using the imagery of light and darkness from 1:5–7. The absence of a return to the theme of sin must be deliberate, and I submit that it is a structural hint of John's later teaching about believers and sin. In chapters 3 and 5, John makes some startling claims:

- "Whoever abides in Him does not sin. Whoever sins has neither seen Him nor known Him." (3:6)
- "He who sins is of the devil, for the devil has sinned from the beginning." (3:8)
- "Whoever has been born of God does not sin, for His seed remains in him; and he cannot sin, because he has been born of God." (3:9)
- We know that no one who is born of God sins; but He who was born of God keeps him, and the evil one does not touch him." (5:18)

We will examine these claims when we get further in the commentary, but for now we can see that 1 John 1:5–2:11 structurally symbolizes the absence of sin in the life of the believer. If we read this section helically,[1] the passage runs as follows:

> God is light, and we must walk in light → what's more, walking in light means loving our brothers.

> If we confess sin, we are forgiven because Jesus is advocate and propitiation → BLANK.

> We know we know him by keeping his commandment → what's more, the old/new commandment is the commandment to love. We must walk as he walked, that is, in obedience, love, and light.

Walking in light and love and obedience produces a life without sin (in the sense John means it). Our sins are forgiven and removed, so we can walk unencumbered. "Sin" is wiped from the text, just as sin is wiped away when we confess.

Several times, John moves from one topic to another with "hook words," a word used at the end of one section that becomes the main theme of the next section ("sin" in 1:7–8; "darkness/light" in 2:8–9). John's use of direct address ("My little children," 2:1; "Beloved," 2:7) also marks off new sections. Though 1:7b (or 1:8)–2:2 forms a distinct unit, it splits in two with the direct address, "My little children" (2:1). Verses 2:1 and 2:7 are parallel not only because both begin with an affectionate direct address to the audience, but also because in both John declares his intention for writing: "I write that you may not sin" (2:1) and "not a new commandment I write to you." (2:7).

Further, 1:8–10 forms a distinct sub-unit. Verses 8 and 10 consist of conditional sentences of similar content and structure:

> A. If we say that we have no sin (v. 8)/have not sinned (v. 10)
> B. we are self-deceived (v. 8)/make Him a liar (v. 10)
> C. truth (v. 8)/word is not in us (v. 10).

---

1. See John Breck, *The Structure of Biblical Language* (2nd ed.; Crestwood, NY: St. Vladimir's Seminary Press, 2008).

Verse 9 has a similar structure, but in content contrasts with the surrounding verses:

A. If we confess our sins
   B. faithful he is and just
      C. to forgive and cleanse.

The parallels are suggestive. Obviously, confession (v. 9, A) contrasts with saying we have not sinned (vv. 8, 10, A). Similarly, God's "faithfulness and righteousness" (v. 9, B) contrasts to self-deceit and making God a liar (vv. 8, 10, B), and this implies a connection between forgiveness of sin/cleansing from unrighteousness (v. 9, C) and the truth or word of God dwelling in us (vv. 8, 10, C).

At the end of this section, John again writes several sentences with parallel syntax and contrasting content. Verse 10 runs:

A. The one who loves his brother
   B. remains in the light
      C. and there is no scandal in him.

Verse 11 has a matching structure, but with contrasting content:

A. The one who hates his brother
   B. is in darkness/walks in darkness
      C. and doesn't know where he goes.

Apart from the C sections, the parallels are obvious. C is clearer when we realize that the Greek word *skandalon* is a "stumbling block." Hatred blinds us, and we trip over the obstacles in our way.

GOD IS LIGHT

1 John 1:5 This is the message we have heard from him and proclaim to you, that God is light, and in him is no darkness at all. 6 If we say we have fellowship with him while we walk in darkness, we lie and do not practice the truth. 7 But if we walk in the light, as he is in the light, we have fellowship with one another, and the blood of Jesus his Son cleanses us from all sin. 8 If we say we have

no sin, we deceive ourselves, and the truth is not in us. [9]If we confess our sins, he is faithful and just to forgive us our sins and to cleanse us from all unrighteousness. [10]If we say we have not sinned, we make him a liar, and his word is not in us.

John passes on a message that he heard from Jesus, the message that God is Light, and in him is no darkness at all (1:5). It naturally follows that if we are going to have fellowship with the God who is light, we must walk in the light. We have already examined the temporal symbolism of darkness and light in chapter 1, but there is more to say.

First, light is associated with life. Light is the first sign of life in the formless void of the original creation, and God has made the world so that without light, everything dies. Plants wither in darkness, and human beings need light to be healthy. In several places, the Bible speaks of the "light of life" (Job 33:30; John 8:12), describes the grave as a place of darkness as well as death (Job 33:30), and refers to stillborn or aborted children as those who "never saw light" (Job 3:16). God is Light, and as such is the source of life (Psalm 4; 56).

Second, the God who shone at the creation sheds light at the exodus, when Israel traveled through the darkness of night but had their way illumined by the light of God's pillar. Yahweh's glory lighted the way for Israel through a dark world (Ex. 13:21; 14:20), and the image of Yahweh's light as a guide for his people is picked up in various psalms (Ps. 18:28; 43; 89:15; 112:4; 119:105). To say that God is Light is to say that he guides his people through the darkness of death and a death-filled world. John appears to have this exodus story in mind: he not only talks about God as Light, but talks about walking in the light, as Israel did, and about the darkness without light that makes people stumble. He could well be describing the fall of thousands of Israelites in the wilderness.

Third, light exposes. Things done in darkness are unknown until they are illuminated, until light shines. According to Psalm 90:8, Yahweh places "our iniquities before You, our secret sins in the light of Your presence." To say that God is Light is to say that he is the

Judge, shining into the shadows and bringing secret things to light. Without light, no one can see, and sight in Scripture is the sense associated with passing judgment. Judgment may seem opposed to life, but the Bible teaches the opposite. God the Light shines to expose and judge, and *thereby* to bring everything to new life.

We should put all these particular associations in a larger biblical perspective that we have already mentioned earlier. The world begins in darkness. When God creates light, he divides darkness and light and organizes them into a pattern of day and night. Each day of creation brings further light, more glory. Throughout history, light and darkness alternate, but someday this cycle will end and there will be no more night (Rev. 21:25; 22:5). The world moves from darkness, to alternation of darkness and light, to absolute eternal light. The God who is Light will be fully revealed only at the end of all things. All that Light means is fully realized only at the consummation. In the future, the fullness of light brings the fullness of life, the full and final judgment, the clarity of climactic revelation. In the end, the Light that has led us on our walk will bring us to our destination. In short, the Light that God is, is the light of the consummation. Light is eschatological, and to say God is Light is to say that God is the God of the future. He already is, and has always been, the fullness of life. Father, Son, and Spirit know, and are known, fully to one another. There are no secret dark corners within him, within them—all is open. To say God is Light is to say that God has already eternally arrived at the consummation toward which creation is moving.

This helps us understand what John means by walking in light. To walk in the light is to walk according to the future Light of the new creation, the new creation that has already begun in the incarnation of the Word of Life. To walk in the light means to walk in hope; to walk in the light is to recognize that this world of mixed darkness and light is temporary; to walk in the light is to set our minds on things ahead, on the world without night that will someday dawn. "Darkness" is the evening of history, the Old Covenant, while "light" is the day of the Lord that comes when the Eternal Light takes flesh (cf. John 1:6–9). The New Covenant is a covenant of light because with it the final age, the age to come, radiates into *this* age.

How is the Old Covenant a covenant of evening that yields to the daytime of the New? Israel was not, to be sure, in utter darkness, any more than night is utterly dark. The moon brings light to the night, and so do the stars. Israel's history took place in the night of the world's history, but Israel had the light of Torah, the light of God's presence, the moonlight of the Temple. Yet the revelation in the Old Covenant was partial and incomplete compared with the sunrise of the Son (cf. Mal. 4:2). God spoke to Israel in many ways and in many times, in many portions in the Old Testament, but these are all flickers of light rather than full day (cf. Heb.1:1–2). Now that the Son has come, he has spoken his final word, a word that cannot be surpassed. He is Light come into the world.

In the Old Covenant, the God of Light dwelt with Israel, but he dwelt behind dark goat's-hair tent curtains, veils, and doors. Yahweh of Hosts was inaccessible to Israel—only the High Priest once a year went into the Most Holy Place to sprinkle blood, and even he did not see the Light of God in any full way. He had to scurry out too quickly to bathe in the light. The Old Covenant was a covenant of veils, which separated the light of God's glory from the people. With the new covenant, the veil is removed and the full light of God shines. The God of Light, the God who is Light, has emerged from hiding and has come among us. As John says, the message of the gospel is that God is Light. He has made himself known as he was not known before. The gospel announces that the God who is Light has stepped from behind the veil, and the whole world is flooded with his light. And the earth shall be full of the glory of the Lord.

Revelation and life itself were incomplete in the Old Covenant. Israel had life with Yahweh, but Israel did not yet have the fullness of the Risen Son and his Spirit; they were not incorporated by the tangible Risen Word of Life into the eternal life of the God who is light. Jesus came to give life, and to give it abundantly.

Not only life and revelation, but judgment also was partial in the Old Testament, because Light had not yet dawned. Under the

Old Covenant, the sins of men were hidden, covered over by the dark of night, covered within Israel by the blood of bulls and goats. During the times of ignorance, Paul tells the Athenians, God overlooked sin, but now that light has come, he declares that all men everywhere should repent (Acts 17:30). In generations gone by, God permitted the nations to go their own ways (Acts 14:16). Before, "in the forbearance of God He passed over the sins previously committed" (Rom. 3:25): no longer. Now the new has come, and the times of ignorance are at an end. There is no place to hide, no escape from the penetrating glance of the Judge of earth.

Still people try. Light has dawned, and yet some people stumble around as if it were night (2:10–11). Those who "walk in darkness" are those who continue to live according to the patterns of the Old Creation, those who continue to maintain the distinctions of the law, or continue to treat God as if he were still hidden behind the veil of the tabernacle, or think they can get away with excuses of ignorance. In John's immediate situation, Judaizers are those who "walk in darkness" and "hate their brothers" by re-erecting holiness and purity laws that divide Jew from Jew and Jew from Gentile. Of course, the light/dark contrast has a broader application. Even if we are not tempted to keep Jewish dietary laws, we can walk in darkness by despising Christian brothers.

Being in the light that is the life of the New Covenant requires more than a profession of faith in Jesus. Several times, John contrasts what people say with what is actually the case (1:6–7; 2:10). We do not have fellowship with Christ merely by *saying* we have fellowship with him. We must not only *say* we have fellowship with Light, but must actually *walk* in the Light, especially by living in fellowship and love with our brothers in the church. God is Light, and his light shines into and through our brothers. We cannot love the light that is God unless we love his light as it shines in our Christian brothers. A profession of fellowship and faith might be falsified by the way we actually walk. If we say we are of the light but continue to live in darkness, we are liars (1:6).

CLEANSED OF SIN

John moves from talking about the God of Light to talking about the walk of those who are in light, and this leads into a consideration of sin. The sequence is not accidental. The Light has come, God has stepped into the open, and as his Light shines we find we are exposed. Our first instinct is to reach for fig leaves. John's readers wanted to retain the fig-leaf aprons made from the blood of bulls and goats in the sacrificial system. More sophisticated, we construct fig leaves with psychological explanations of sin or the time-tested, ancient method of blame-shifting.

None of these subterfuges works. Exposure is inherent in the gospel. We can't confess the gospel that God is Light, and that the Light has come, and still cling to darkness. If we cover over our sins, pretend they don't exist, refuse to admit them, then we are liars, and worse than liars: we make God a liar (1:10). According to John, the way of escape is not to cower in the shadows but to confess sin openly. Paradoxically, the way of covering is the way of exposure. We have fellowship with the light by accepting the exposure, agreeing with it, submitting to it, and confessing our sins (1:8–9). We have fellowship with the light by bathing in the light, even as it exposes all our blemishes and pock marks. Only one covering works when the Light of God confronts us, the cover that the Light himself provides: the blood of Jesus.

Surely, John would have agreed that we receive cleansing by faith, but that is not the way he puts things. The blood of Jesus cleanses us insofar as we are walking in the light, which means having fellowship with one another (cf. 2:10–11). Note the sequence of clauses in 1:7: when we walk in the light, we have fellowship with one another; and when we have fellowship with one another, Jesus' blood cleanses our sin. Walking in the light is a prerequisite for cleansing. We can be cleansed only by living by the light of the future that has dawned, which means, practically, living by the standards and commandments of the New Covenant, particularly living in communion with fellow believers. We find cleansing by our adherence to the communion of the church—not, as Jews and

Judaizers claimed, in temple sacrifices, which could never take away sin (Heb. 10:4). And not, as many pseudo-zealots have it, by separating from the impure sinners who constitute the church. Cleansing comes by remaining in fellowship with those very people. How, we are led to ponder, can we find cleansing when for the last several hundred years we have institutionalized our fraternal hatreds? How can we find cleansing when we have institutionalized darkness?

The coming of light is frightening when our deeds are evil. We do not want God to peer into the nooks and crannies of our hearts and lives. We want to keep some secret place for our very own. We want to nurture some monstrous thing in the dark places, but that is not the way of life. Light is life, and that means life is only possible when we submit to God's scrutiny and judgment, when we allow ourselves to be exposed by the Light that is God, when we agree with that exposure and freely confess our sins. Don't think that you can have life in darkness. You cannot. Life only comes through the shining of the light. Abundant life lies on the far side of the judgment that the light brings. Only on that distant shore can we walk in the light of the living, only then will be know the light of life.

ADVOCATE AND COVER

1 John 2:1My little children, I am writing these things to you so that you may not sin. But if anyone does sin, we have an advocate with the Father, Jesus Christ the righteous. 2He is the propitiation for our sins, and not for ours only but also for the sins of the whole world.

As he begins chapter 2, John is still talking about sin and how to handle sin. He writes so his readers will avoid sin (2:1) , but John recognizes that believers will sin, and denying sin is lying, an additional sin (1:8). In chapter 1, he urges us to confess our sins in order to be cleansed, and in chapter 2, John adds some details about how *God* has dealt with our sin. How is it that when we confess our sins, God is faithful and just to forgive sins? How can forgiveness of sins be *just*? How can God just overlook our sin and put it behind us as far as the east is from the west? And, especially, how is this "overlooking" consistent with the New Covenant's emphasis on exposure? How can the New Covenant be a covenant of both light and cleansing, a covenant of light *and* life?

John explains by saying that Jesus is the Paraclete (*parakleton*). John applies to Jesus the same word Jesus uses to describe the Spirit (John 14:16), and the word refers to a defense attorney. We can be confident before the Father because we have a public advocate, a lawyer for our defense, before the Father's throne in heaven. This is one of the great blessings of the New Covenant. In the Old Covenant, Satan was in the throne room of the Father, and presented his case before God (Job 1–2; Zech. 3). Satan is an adversary, and particularly an adversary at law. He is an accuser, a prosecuting attorney, but Satan the accuser has been cast down through the death, resurrection, and ascension of Jesus. In his place we have a Paraclete. The coming of the New Covenant doesn't mean that God shuts down the courtroom. It means that he adds an officer to the court.

Verse 2 describes the work of Jesus as propitiation (*hilasmos*). As an abstract idea, to propitiate is to pacify anger. Jesus turns away the wrath of God by his obedience unto death. Wrath is poured out against sinful humanity, and that wrath has to be satisfied if we are going to be at peace with God. This has been a troubling doctrine for many in the modern world, mainly because it suggests that God is a quick-tempered tyrant. This is too large a question to address in detail here, but a few points may be made.

There is no doubt that the God of the Bible is a God who becomes angry against sin and sinful people (Lev. 26:28; Num. 16:46; Deut. 9:7–8; 1 Sam. 28:18; 2 Kings 22:13; Matt. 3:7; Rom. 1:18; 2:5–8; 9:22). And there is also no doubt from Scripture that sinners must be rescued from God's wrath if we hope to have communion and fellowship with him. Human beings have become sinners, and thus enemies of God, and need to be reconciled to him, and, more importantly, he with us. This reconciliation demands that we be "saved from the wrath of God" (Rom. 5:8–10). Jesus is the one who rescues us from the coming wrath of God, the wrath of judgment that Paul details in Romans 2. Romans 5:9 says that we are saved from the wrath of God "through *Him*," that is, through Jesus, and in 1 Thessalonians 1:10 Paul writes that Jesus is the one who rescues us from the "coming wrath" (cf. Matt. 3:7; Luke 3:7). Jesus rescues us from wrath by absorbing that wrath in himself, by drinking the cup that his Father offers (Mark 14:36), the cup of wrath (cf. Ps. 75:8; Is. 51:17–23; Jer. 25:15–29; Eze. 23:31–34).[2] The Word of Life assumes to himself our humanity, the humanity that is under wrath, and absorbs that wrath in himself. Thus, he is a propitiation.

Summarizing the argument of Romans 3, Simon Gathercole writes, "when we come to Romans 3:20, all are under judgment, and doomed to face God's wrath. By the time we reach 3:27–31, however, Paul is talking of people being justified. How is it, then, that sin and wrath have been dealt with?"[3] Romans 3:25–26 provide the answer: the transition occurs because God has set Jesus out as "a propitiation (*hilastērion*) through faith in His blood." Jesus' death deals with sin and the wrath of God against sin. N. T. Wright likewise accepts that "the lexical history of the word *hilastērion* is sufficiently flexible to admit of particular nuances in different contexts," but argues that "Paul's context here demands that the word not only retain its sacrificial overtones . . . but that it carry the note of propitiation of divine wrath—with, of course, the corollary that sins are expiated."[4]

Yet this can still seem odd. God sends Jesus because he loves the world (John 3:16), so how can the Son's death be a solution to God's wrath? If he already loves us before he sends his Son, why does the Son have to deal with wrath at all? Paul makes it clear that there is no conflict in his mind between the love of God and his wrath: God demonstrated his love in the fact that Jesus died for us; his death is the foundation of our justification, and having been justified we also

---

2. Michael Ovey et. al., *Pierced for Our Transgressions: Rediscovering the Glory of Penal Substitution* (Crossway, 2007), 137.

3. Quoted in Ovey, 81.

4. Wright, *Romans* in *The New Interpreter's Bible* (Nashville: Abingdon Press, 2002), vol. 10, 476.

hope for salvation from the future wrath of God, through the same Jesus who shed his blood for us (Rom. 5:8–9). God sends his Son because he loves; but that Son delivers from wrath.

In contemporary theology, the problem is often posed as a problem of trinitarian theology. What is happening on the cross? Is the Father angry with the Son? Is the Father joined by the Spirit in being angry at the Son? Or, is the eternal Son pouring out wrath alongside the Father and Spirit on Jesus the man? We are faced with a dilemma: either the Trinity is divided, or the divine and human natures of Jesus are divided. Either there is a division between Father and Son, such that it appears that the Father is angry and the Son is self-giving in his love; or, if the Son joins the Father in punishing sin on the cross, the Son seems to be expressing wrath toward himself, or pouring out wrath on his human nature.[5]

To make sense of propitiation in a trinitarian framework, we need to recognize that wrath is not an expression of hatred but of jilted love. According to the *Theological Dictionary of the New Testament*,

> At the back of every individual prophetic charge, whether it refers to the cultus or to social injustice, to a policy which trusts in armaments and alliances, or even to the worship of other gods, there stands finally the one great complaint, namely, that the people has forgotten its God, turned from him, and despised His love. This is the deepest root of the concept of wrath, and in this light one can understand the overwhelming force of the message. It is Yahweh's wounded love which awakens His wrath. . . . If Yahweh's love is not reciprocated by the people, if it turns aside to other gods, His jealousy burns. This finds expression in wrath . . . and it casts out Israel, the unfaithful wife.[6]

Jealousy is a sense of ownership in another, and the determination to keep what is ours. When what is ours turns away, jealous

---

5. The problems are not as dire as this, as explained in *Pierced for Our Transgressions*, 126–32. Still, the discussion in that book is not entirely satisfactory.
6. (10 vols.; Grand Rapids: Eerdmans, 1981), vol. 5, 403.

love burns as wrath (Num. 25:11; Ezek. 16:38; 23:25; 36:26; Nah. 1:2; Zech. 8:2).

The connection of wrath to the jealousy of possessive love helps to resolve the apparent trinitarian difficulties of the notion of propitiation. God is jealous, a God who defends his own name, and this jealousy flowers out in a trinitarian fashion. The Father loves the Son because the Son is the Son of the Father. The Father takes up the Son's cause, defending the beloved Son with a jealous wrath against creatures who rebel against the Word by whom all things were made. Likewise, the Son loves the Father, and when the Father is slandered or attacked, the Son takes up the Father's cause and defends the Father.

In this framework, to say Jesus is the propitiation for our sins means that he has taken this wrath on himself, and the jealous wrath by which the Father defends his Son is poured out on the Son. Having taken on the humanity that has rebelled against the Father, the Son turns the other cheek, and suffers for all the sins that humanity has committed *against him*. This is the double restitution that satisfies the justice of God: first, that the Son suffers the original offense, and second that the Son endures the jealous wrath against those who committed the offense. The Father displays his love by sending the Son to enact the strange justice of God, the justice of the cross, the justice of turning the cheek.

COVERING

In 1 John 2, the word has not only this abstract sense of propitiation but also a more concrete sense. In the Septuagint, the related word *hilastērion* refers exclusively to the cover of the ark of the covenant (Ex. 25:17–22 [seven times]; 31:7; 35:12; 38:5–8 [four times]; Lev. 16:2, 13–15 [four times]; Num. 7:89). Elsewhere, the word refers to the capitals of pillars (Amos 9:1), and to a portion of a visionary altar (Ezek. 43:14, 17, 20). It is never used in the abstract sense of propitiation, and in one of the two uses in the New Testament it also refers to the ark cover (Heb. 9:5). To be sure, the related verb, *hilaskomai*, refers not to objects but to attitudes. In Exodus

32:14, it describes Yahweh's "repentance" for the wrath he planned against Israel, and in 2 Kings 5:18 it has the sense of pardon or forgive (cf. 2 Kings 24:4; Pss. 25:11; 65:3; 78:38; 79:9). In these passages, the word does not mean precisely "propitiate," though, given the threat of Yahweh's wrath evident in the context, the word might imply pacification of God's anger.

The specific word used by John is *hilasmon*, used only a handful of times in the Septuagint. In Leviticus 25:9, it means "atonement" in the phrase "day of atonement," *Yom Kippur*, and it again translates the Hebrew word for "atonement" in Numbers 5:9. It means "forgiveness" in Psalm 130:4, and in 1 Chronicles 28:20, a passage not found in the Hebrew Massoretic Text, David lists the various zones of the Temple: "the house, and its treasury, and the upper chambers, and the inner store-rooms, and the place of propitiation (*oikon tou hilasmou*), and the plan of the house of the LORD." The phrase "house of *hilasmon*" could refer to the Most Holy Place, where the rites of the day of atonement were performed, or could refer to the Temple strictly speaking, since the rest of the list describes adjoining buildings and storage areas. In Ezekiel 44:27, the word translates the Hebrew *hattat*, the word for "sin offering" or "purification offering."

The connotations of *hilastērion* have been obscured by English translations that attempt to capture the notion of propitiation even when describing the cover of the ark. Many English Bibles use the word "mercy-seat" for the ark cover, and others use "propitiatory." The Hebrew term behind these Greek and English translations is *kapporet*, from *kipper*, the word for atonement. Fundamentally, that word means not propitiation or mercy or even atonement but simply "cover." The ark-cover is called a *kapporet* because that is what it does: it *covers* the ark.

This is what Jesus does. Like the tabernacle as a whole, the ark was a miniature cosmos. Its feet were planted on the ground, and the hollow coffer of the ark contained God's gifts to humanity—Torah, manna, and Aaron's staff; wisdom, life, and authority. At the top of the ark were solid gold cherubim upon which Yahweh was enthroned, as he is enthroned amidst angelic armies in heaven. Between the earth and the throne of Yahweh was the "covering," which represented the firmament-footstool of Yahweh, the pavement like sapphire (Ex. 24:10) through which Yahweh views his people. To say Jesus is the *hilasmon* means that he is the ark covering, which is the screen, the new firmament, through which the Father views the world. This is the ark cover on which the High Priest sprinkled blood on the Day of Atonement. Since the incarnation of the Son, the Father looks on his world through the living veil of Jesus, through the firmament of his Son.

SINS OF THE WORLD

This helps to explain the universalism of John's statement in verse 2. If *hilasmon* is interpreted as "propitiation," this verse teaches that Jesus turns God's wrath away from the whole of humanity. If that is true, then universal salvation seems to follow naturally. Why would God send people to hell if Jesus has propitiated wrath against everyone? The problem is exacerbated for Calvinists, who believe in a definite atonement. Definite atonement means that Jesus died to secure the salvation for his people, his Bride, his elect. His death was utterly efficacious. Everyone for whom Jesus died will be eternally saved. There is no conflict between the electing plan of God, which specifies a particular people as the chosen from all ages, and the atonement, through which Jesus achieves that salvation.

John is saying here that Jesus is the propitiation for the sins of the whole world, and John is not the only New Testament writer to say this:

> It is a trustworthy statement deserving full acceptance. For it is for this we labor and strive, because we have fixed our hope on *the living God, who is the Savior of all men, especially of believers.* (1 Tim. 4:10)

> Urge bondslaves to be subject to their own masters in everything, to be well-pleasing, not argumentative, not pilfering, but showing all good faith so that they will adorn the doctrine of God our

Savior in every respect. For the grace of God has appeared, *bringing salvation to all men*, instructing us to deny ungodliness and worldly desires and to live sensibly, righteously and godly in the present age, looking for the blessed hope and the appearing of the glory of our great God and Savior, Christ Jesus. (Titus 2:11)

Jesus is called the "Savior of the world." (1 John 4:14)

The cross has multiple intentions. Jesus died to secure salvation for his sheep (John 10), which is his Bride and Body (Eph. 5), but he also died and rose again to be the "firmament-covering" for the whole world. Jesus is set forth as a *hilastērion* through his blood for the whole creation.[7] Since the death and resurrection of Jesus, the Father regards the whole world and its sins through the firmament-cover that is Jesus Christ. Though the age of light has come, the Light itself provides covering for us, so that we both walk in the Light and have our sins cleansed and removed.

For believers, this has particular significance. Because Jesus is the cover, there is no condemnation—*no* condemnation! God's wrath is turned away, he forgives us wholly and freely. He looks at us through the blood of Jesus. Jesus is defending us, and Jesus is not only the Righteous, but the Beloved Son. Will the Father deny the requests of his Son as he defends us before the Father? Believers often think and act as if this is not true, as if God is still angry with us. The car won't start or we have a flat tire; our children get sick

---

7. James Jordan writes in a personal communication, "I cannot for the life of me see 'propitiation' or any other abstract noun as correct here. It's the Ark-Cover. How could any 1st. c. reader have thought anything else? Jesus is the New Ark-Cover. The Ark-Cover, as is plain in Exodus 25, signifies the firmament. Jesus is the new Protecting firmament over the whole world and all humanity, through His blood. The blood was displayed on the Ark-Cover-firmament. Now it's displayed on Jesus. When the Father looks at the world, He sees the firmament (Jesus) and blood on it. That's propitiation, yes. But Jesus is more than the propitiation. He's the Ark-Cover. God put the Warbow in the firmament as a sign to Noah of universal peace and a universal covenant. Jesus is the new firmament, the new Warbow. Is He any less a universal sign, for all humans as long as they live under the firmament?"

or the boss is bearing down on us at work. Our first reaction is often to think that God is out to get us, that he is hostile to us, and that he gets his kicks out of setting traps for us because he enjoys pratfalls, or worse, that he still condemns us.

Against all this, the Bible says there is *no condemnation* for those who are in Christ. Not a *little* condemnation, not condemnation in the future. God doesn't condemn us at all. Light—the light of the Judge—has exposed us, but those who are in Jesus have a covering. This is the good news announced in baptism, in the declaration of forgiveness, in the Supper of the Lord. We are called only to believe it and walk in this confidence: *no* condemnation.

KNOWING THAT WE KNOW

1 John 2:3 And by this we know that we have come to know him, if we keep his commandments. ⁴Whoever says "I know him" but does not keep his commandments is a liar, and the truth is not in him, ⁵but whoever keeps his word, in him truly the love of God is perfected. By this we may know that we are in him: ⁶whoever says he abides in him ought to walk in the same way in which he walked. ⁷Beloved, I am writing you no new commandment, but an old commandment that you had from the beginning. The old commandment is the word that you have heard. ⁸At the same time, it is a new commandment that I am writing to you, which is true in him and in you, because the darkness is passing away and the true light is already shining. ⁹Whoever says he is in the light and hates his brother is still in darkness. ¹⁰Whoever loves his brother abides in the light, and in him there is no cause for stumbling. ¹¹But whoever hates his brother is in the darkness and walks in the darkness, and does not know where he is going, because the darkness has blinded his eyes.

Our lives must be characterized by obedience to God's commandments and by imitation of Jesus. That is what John goes on to emphasize. He knows that we will sin, and he tells us how to deal with our sins when we commit them. But the thrust of his letter is to insist that Christians must be obedient if they are to be real Christians at all. If we claim to be disciples of Jesus but consistently and impenitently disobey him, we are liars (2:4). It really is that simple.

As soon as commandments come into the picture, Protestants get scared of works-righteousness, the law, a confusion of law and gospel. But the consistent teaching of the New Testament is that obedience is as essential for the Christian as it was for the Jew. John is very severe in 2:4: "You say you're in a relationship of friendship with God, that you know him, that you are his son, and yet disobey his commandments. That's a lie." Disobedient Christians lie with their lives, whatever the truth of their words. John is not afraid to talk about obedience as a *requirement* for Christians.

Obedience is not only required but also, John says, a means for knowing that we know him (2:3). What is this "knowing that we know"? Though he uses the same word twice (*ginōskō*), John is obviously using "know" in two different senses, or at two different levels. The second meaning is easier to grasp. When John uses know the second time, he means "be in a relationship of love and friendship." John is talking about knowing God in the way that Adam knew Eve, in intimate love and friendship. Keeping God's commandments is a means of assuring us that we are in a loving relationship with God through Christ.

What does the first "know" mean? It could mean "being intellectually convinced of." On this reading, "knowing that we know" means being intellectually persuaded that we are in a relationship of friendship with God. John would therefore be saying that we become intellectually convinced that we are in a right relation with God by obeying his commandments. We might think of obedience as part of a checklist. Using the checklist, we examine ourselves, knowing that we are in a friendly relationship. Historically, this has sometimes taken the form of what is called the "practical syllogism": God says that those who obey truly know him; I evaluate myself, and find that I obey; therefore, I truly know him.

There are problems with this way of understanding John. One problem is that we can always find considerable disobedience mixed in with our obedience. If we step outside ourselves and try to evaluate our performance, we are always going to discover blemishes and flaws in the crystal, as John knows. At the same time, this kind of process can also lead to presumption: I look at my performance, and I think I'm doing just fine, so I conclude I must be a real Christian. I tick off the commandments: no adultery this week, check; no murders, check; no extortion or fraud, check. I must be doing well. Now I know that I know him. We forget how subtle sin is, and how desperately sinful and self-deceived we can still be.

John is not talking about this at all. "Know" could also mean "be assured of" or "experiencing fully" in a more existential sense. We use the word the English word "know" in this sense frequently. I never knew beer until I tried Guinness; I never knew love until I met my wife; I never knew joy until I had children. We might know all about beer—the ingredients, the process of beer-making, the percentage of carbs and fats in the final product—and still not *know* beer in the experiential sense. Knowing beer in this sense means appreciating it fully, experiencing beer in the fullest manner. We might have known a great many details about many love stories, but if we have never experienced love we don't *know* love.

I suggest that John's first "know" means both "fully experience" and "be assured of." To know that we have come to know God means that we have a *full experience* of being in a right relationship with him, and that we are *assured* of being in a right relationship with him. This has an intellectual component, but John's focus is more existential. To put it into our own language, "we know we have come to know him" means "we have a full experience and existential assurance of a loving, intimate relationship with God."

How do we achieve this full experience, this assurance? John says it comes through keeping the commandments, but keeping the commandments is not part of a checklist or a syllogism. It is the *pathway* to full and assured experience of God's love and favor and friendship. For John, obedience itself—not knowledge of obedience–is the means to reach assurance and the full experience of friendship with God. For the practical syllogism, reflection on and evaluation of our obedience is the pathway of assurance. John does not say we come to full experience and assurance by standing back and reflecting on our performance. We come to full experience and assurance by and through, in, with, and under, keeping God's commandments. Knowing that we know comes by *keeping* the commandments, not by *knowing* that we keep the commandments or by *thinking* about keeping the commandments.

If you are struggling with assurance, if you don't experience the joy, delight, energy, life, and power that comes from knowing God, from fellowship with him, or the assurance of knowing that you know him, the answer is to repent. Confess your sins through the Advocate, and stop doing what you're doing. If you can't stop doing what you're doing on your own, ask for help from other believers and pray for a fuller measure of the Spirit. Start walking as Jesus walked. Start keeping the commandments of God. That is the pathway to assurance; that is the way to know that you know him.

John describes this somewhat differently in 2:5: whoever keeps his word, in him the love of God is perfected. What is the love of God? Our love for God, or God's love for us? 1 John 4:12 (which is in the chiastically-matching section) says that perfected love comes when God abides in us. In that verse, John is talking about God's love for us, personified in the Spirit, remaining in us so that his love for us will come to perfection. John means the same thing in 2:4. The love of God that is perfected is the love of God for us, brought to us through the Spirit, coming to perfection through keeping the commandments. Through much of Scripture, perfection does not mean sinlessness, but rather maturity. The love of God comes to full and complete expression in us as we keep his commandments. Obedience is the path of assurance; it is also the path of maturity.

While the Ten Words provide a good summary of God's commandments, John highlights what he describes as a "new commandment." John no doubt has Jesus' "new commandment" in mind (John 13:34; 15:12; cf. 1 John 2:8), the commandment to believe in Jesus and to love one another with the same self-giving love Jesus showed for us (cf. 1 John 3:22–24; 4:21). At the same time, he describes this commandment as an "old commandment" and the "word you heard" (2:7). The "word you have heard" is linked with the message from the apostles, the message of the gospel (1:5). John, in short, characterizes the gospel as a "new commandment," another indication that he does not polarize law and gospel.

The difference between Old and New is *not* that in the Old Covenant, people had to obey God, and we no longer have to. The difference is that God promises his Spirit to enable us to obey. That is the glory of the New Covenant—not freedom to disobey, but freedom from sin, the true freedom of obedience.

Importantly, John connects knowledge with loving one another. The connection is not obvious, especially to modern Americans. We Americans like to pretend we are self-made men and women. We don't need nobody's help, don't tread on me, we'll go it alone if only you leave us alone, thank you very much. My life, my body, my person are mine and mine alone. We think that we can make our way through life as independent contractors. As a result, we Americans are particularly apt to the delusion that our relationships have no effect on the way our lives go. John makes it clear that this is not the case. If we hate our brothers; if we are full of envy, anger, malice, bitterness, wrath, and clamor; if our speech is sprinkled with gossip and lies and slander—then John says our way is not going to be easy. Hatred is the way of darkness, and in darkness we can't help but trip and fall (2:10–11). Hatred makes us stupid.

John is not being metaphorical. If we are unforgiving and bitter toward our husband or wife, we will be incapable of understanding them. My wife might do everything to make me happy and comfortable, but if I am angry with her I will see it as an insult. Malice and wrath literally blind us in our relationships. We walk in darkness and do not know what makes us stumble.

You want to know God's will for your life, but everything seems murky and hidden. God has given you no clear path. You seem to be faltering in the darkness, tripping over everything and generally lurching through life. Why doesn't God give you some clear direction? Where's the light switch?

Here's a suggestion: if you feel like you're groping through a moonless night, examine how you're living with your brothers, particularly those nearest to you. How do you talk to your kids? Have you had fights with every roommate you've ever had? Are you treating your wife as you would like to be treated? Do you love your brothers and sisters—genuinely love them, or are you at best indifferent? If you want the darkness to yield to the dawn, if you want to know where the Lord is leading you, turn to the Lord and ask him to give you the power to repent and love your brothers and sisters. For "the path of the righteous is like the first gleam of dawn, shining ever brighter to the full light of day. But the way of the wicked is deep darkness; they don't even know what makes them stumble."

5

DO NOT LOVE THE WORLD
1 John 2:12–17

This short section of John's gospel is one of the most influential passages in the entire New Testament. In *Confessions*, Augustine used these verses to organize his thoughts about the seductions and temptations of the world. For him, the lust of the eyes not only includes the temptation of beauty that distracts us from the beauty of God, but also our strange fascination with horrible things. The lust of the eyes is at work when we slow down and look at the wreckage of a car accident as much as it is when our eyes linger on a centerfold. Lust of the eyes includes vain curiosity, the aimless quest for useless trivia that characterizes many intellectuals, ancient and modern.

Augustine describes the pride of life as the desire to be the object of attention:

The temptation is to wish to be feared or loved by people for no reason other than the joy derived from such power, which is no joy at all. It is a wretched life, and vanity is repulsive. . . . When we try to amass such approval [from men], we are caught off our guard. We cease to find our joy in your truth and place it in the deceitfulness of men. It becomes our pleasure to be loved and feared not for your sake, but instead of you. By this method, the Enemy makes people resemble himself, united with him not in loving concord but in sharing a common punishment. (*Confessions*, Book 10)

When answering the question "Why do we sin?" Thomas Aquinas cited 1 John 2:16. His answer was that evil desire—what he called "concupiscence"—brings about sin. Some desires are natural and legitimate, such as the desires for food, drink, and sex, but we should not idolize these things, and any excessive desire for good things is lust or concupiscence. Some evil desires don't focus on sensible things, on bodily feelings, but rather are what Aquinas calls "spiritual concupiscence," desire for things that we perceive or imagine. Money doesn't bring any bodily pleasure in itself, and the bodily pleasure of fine clothing is limited. Many pursue these things because they stimulate imagination. Pride of life is the excessive desire for excellence and reputation. Following Augustine, Aquinas concludes that "all passions that are a cause of sin can be reduced to these three"—the desire of the flesh, the desire of the eyes, and the boastful pride of life (*Summa Theologiae*, I–II, q. 77).

These meditations have permanent relevance to Christians. What Augustine says about "pride of life" involves, for Augustine and probably for John, the love of celebrity, of attention, of approval. Someone motivated by pride of life strives for fame and reputation. He wants to be on every magazine cover, and wants everyone to know his name. Sound familiar? We have a culture of celebrity that would have left Augustine speechless. A celebrity, as Daniel Boorstin said, is someone famous for being famous—not for any contribution or achievement. A celebrity's life goal is to retain public attention, to satisfy the "pride of life." Can you say Paris Hilton?

We would never want that kind of life, would we? We are too pious. But have you never been tempted to think, "It'd be *sooo* cool to be famous. It would be awesome to have random people asking for an autograph, to have sexy groupies hitting on me." Have you never stolen a glance at *People* magazine or the *National Enquirer*, not to mock it but because you're curious about the lifestyles of the rich and famous? Have you never bought something—a pair of basketball shoes, or a brand of beer—because you saw a celebrity wearing or using it? Much of the advertising industry and our mass media as well promote celebrity and entice us to pattern our lives after these celebrities, and thus is an industry devoted to promoting "pride of life." Advertisement gives us the illusion that we participate in the fame of the famous, that we can bathe in the glow of their glory if only we wear their brands. If anything, John's warning is more important in our day than it was in his, because the "world" is so much with us, penetrating into our lives in ways that it couldn't before modern communications technologies.

CHILDREN, FATHERS, YOUNG MEN

1 John 2:12I am writing to you, little children,
because your sins are forgiven for his name's sake.
13I am writing to you, fathers,
because you know him who is from the beginning.
I am writing to you, young men,
because you have overcome the evil one.
I write to you, children,
because you know the Father.
14I write to you, fathers,
because you know him who is from the beginning.
I write to you, young men,
because you are strong,
and the word of God abides in you,
and you have overcome the evil one.

Before he warns against conformity to the world, John states his purpose for writing to different groups within the church. Verses

12 through 14 raise many questions and give few answers. What, for instance, are these verses doing here? They stand out as a separate section, with little connection to what goes before and after. John has been trundling along talking about walking in light and loving the brothers, and then lurches into the exhortation not to love the world. In the middle, he digresses to address the readers directly. He addresses his readers frequently (e.g., 2:1, 18), and he regularly stops to state his reasons for writing (e.g., 1:4; 2:1). But why here?

Equally puzzling is the list of the addressees, the "children," "fathers," and "young men." Are they different groups within the church? Or are they different descriptions of the same group? If they are the same, why use different descriptions? And if they are different groups, who belongs to these groups? Are these literal age groups? Or do the references to children, young men, and fathers have a spiritual reference to maturity in the faith? Plus, why does John repeat himself? He says the very same thing to fathers twice, and addresses children and young men twice, though he says different things about them each time.

Part of the answer depends on the overall structure of the opening section of 1 John. As noted in the structural analysis in chapter 2, 2:12–14 picks up a number of terms and themes that appear at the very beginning of John's letter. Verse 13 is the second time John uses the word "beginning" (*archē*) since the opening verse (cf. 2:7). Verse 2:14 is the third time in the book that John mentions the "word" (cf. 1:1, 10), and after this he doesn't repeat it until 3:18. The prologue (1:1–4) ends with a declaration about John's intentions in writing, and he uses the verb *graphō* six times in 2:12–14 (though see 2:1, 7–8). Further, 1:1 and 2:16 are the only verses in the letter that use the noun "eyes," and both 1:1 and 2:17 use a form of "eternal." In short, though 2:12–17 seems to fit uneasily in its setting in the letter, John has been careful to integrate the section into the larger pattern of his letter.

Why does John repeat himself? Of course the repetition is not exact, either in the terminology for the groups or for the reasons he gives for writing. John climaxes this double-three structure with another triple structure in verse 14:

Group	Reason for writing
First cycle	
little children (*teknia*)	sins are forgiven
fathers	you know him who is from beginning
young men	you have overcome the evil one
Second cycle	
children (*paidia*)	you know the Father
fathers	you know him who is from beginning
young men	you are strong
	the word abides in you
	you have overcome the evil one

In short: three groups, each of which is addressed twice; each is associated with some spiritual achievement or benefit, which can be summed as "forgiveness," "knowledge," and "victory"; and this double-triad structure expands into a triad of triads with the triple commendation of young men at the end.

John organizes his thoughts in threes very frequently in the letter. In 2:16 he describes "all that is in the world" under the headings of "lust of the flesh, lust of the eyes, and boastful pride of life." In 5:8, he says, "there are three that bear witness, the Spirit and the water and the blood, and these three are in agreement." This last reference is a clue to the purpose of the triads and repetitions. Under the law, the truth of a statement was established by multiple witnesses (Deut. 17:6; 19:15; cf. Matt. 18:16), and in the Bible, the legal requirement of two or three witnesses becomes a stylistic device. When Jesus says "Truly, truly I say to you," he is using an oath form, repeating the word truly as a "two-witness" idiom. John is doing the same in 5:8, and in 2:12–14, he repeats himself to call on multiple witnesses.

What about the different groups? The best option seems to be this: John's "children" are all the believers in the churches he is writing to, those with whom he has a "paternal" relation as a father in the faith. He frequently addresses the entire church as "children" (cf. 2:1, 28; 3:7, 18; 4:4; 5:21). In these verses, he uses two different words for "children." The first (*teknia*) is from a word that is etymologically linked with the verb for bearing children, and emphasizes (slightly) the common nature that children have with parents. Children of the same parents share their parents' DNA. By using this word, John is emphasizing that all the children of God bear a family resemblance to their common Father. As he says in the next chapter, those who are his children are all of the same family because they are all "born of God" (3:9). The other word for "children" (*paideia*) emphasizes discipline or training. The members of the church are children and siblings not only because they have the same Father but because they are all subjected to the same discipline and teaching, formed by the same culture of the church. They are brothers and sisters by nurture, as well as by nature. All of the children who make up the church share in the same blessings, which John describes as "forgiveness" and "knowing the Father." These are the primary blessings the children of God enjoy in the New Covenant. Sin is an obstacle to knowing God, but as John has already said, Jesus is the Advocate and propitiation for our sins, so that if we confess our sins God will forgive and cleanse us. He "looses" us from bondage, releases us from sin's guilt and punishment and power. He will liberate us from sin and all of sin's effects because of Jesus. Both of these gifts are the result of God's emergence from hiding: because he has come to us in his Son, we know the Father, and his coming as the tangible Word also achieves forgiveness.

Within this family of children, John distinguishes two groups, and each of these groups has a particular strength. Elsewhere in the New Testament, "fathers" is never used of all Christians. It is sometimes used of the church's Israelite ancestors (Rom. 11:28; 2 Pet. 3:4), and at least once in Paul's letters of mature believers, teachers, or leaders of the church (1 Cor. 4:15). John uses it in the latter sense.

John says that the fathers or leaders have also come to know the Father who is from the beginning (1 John 2:13, 14). John addresses younger believers as "young men," and reminds them that they have overcome the devil through the word of God and the power of Jesus (2:13, 14). These categories might well have reference to actual age. Most of the "fathers" or "leaders" of the early church would have been older men, who not only had long experience as Christians but long experience in life.

Whatever the particulars, several things emerge from these verses. First, the church is a family. The abundance of family terminology applied to the church in the New Testament is remarkable. The church as a whole is our mother (Gal. 4:26), and Paul describes himself in various places as both the "father" and the "mother" of the believers to whom he brought the gospel (Gal. 3:19). Christians are all "brothers" of one another because all are sons and daughters of the Father, and all are siblings of Jesus. Some in the church are described as being immature "children" who need milk and are not prepared for solid food (Heb. 5:11–14).

Kin terminology has important implications for how we live together as a church. How much would it take for you to renounce fellowship with your brother or sister or child? Think of how wrenching it is when parents and children are at odds with each other. Think of the lengths you pursue to maintain some tie with a brother who is drifting away. Now think about how you treat a brother in the church who drifts away. Often, someone makes a single cutting remark, and we break fellowship with him. John is dealing with a similarly divided church, and insists that we are all members of one another, brothers and sisters who should treat one another as kin.

This also has implications for how we think of families. In some senses, the church can be conceived as a collection of family units, but more fundamentally, the church is not a collection of discrete families but a family to itself, a new extended family. Some earnest and faithful Christians today emphasize the importance of family but distort it by making the family the center of God's purposes and program. The family is central, but the family that is central is the family of the church. Obviously, these families frequently overlap, and that overlap indicates how we are to live in the home. Wives and husbands and children are fellow believers as well as members of the same blood family. Because of that, we are called to treat them with the same forbearance and love that we show to other believers.

Second, like a family, the church is made of people of diverse levels of maturity, each of which has its particular strengths and gifts. A healthy church requires and welcomes the contributions of all. A church of young men would be vigorous, but potentially unwise; on the other hand, settled fathers in the faith benefit from the zeal and creative questioning of the young.

One of the key features of the "world" of our day, the world that we are not to love, is the exaltation of youth. Young is good, and old is bad and uncool. An old song, an old style of shoes, an old car are bad; sometimes retro is cool, but retro is cool because retro is new, youthful. Liking retro is not the same as respect for elders. Respect for elders is a constant theme in the Bible. We are to honor parents, and that honor is to be extended to all who are in parental roles toward us. We are to rise in the presence of the gray head, and show respect for the aged. This is particularly important in the church. The fathers that John talks about know the one who has been from the beginning. This might refer to Jesus as the one who comes from the *Archē*, the Father, or it might be a reference to the Father. Knowing one is knowing the other. John emphasizes that the experience and knowledge of fathers is old, stable, permanent.

Aging is, or ought to be, growth in wisdom. When you're young, you haven't been through many trials and difficulties. Your parents have protected you from the hardest demands of the world, and when you face your first real challenge in life—an illness, inability to find a job, failure at school, frustrated love—you are tempted to think that it's the end of everything. Older men and women, however, have seen a lot. They know that the Lord is from the beginning, that Jesus Christ is the same yesterday, today, and forever, that the Lord delivers from *all* evil and danger. They know this not only because it's in the Bible but because they have lived through trials and come out the other side. They have lived through beginnings, middles, and ends of troubles. Things that cause distress among the young do not distress the old, and the young need to learn from the old to be anxious for nothing.

John writes to the young men because of their strength, which leads them to victory over the "evil one," over Satan. John is obviously depicting the life of the young men as a life of battle, but this strength is not an inherent strength. As John says in verse 14, the strength of young men comes only by abiding in the word of God. The Word of Scripture, the word preached, the Word made flesh: all of these senses are in play. Young men are strong and victorious in battle through abiding in, remaining in the word of God. John is also saying that the lives of young men, the lives of Christians in the prime of life, involve not battle but victory. Living as a Christian means overcoming the evil one, the devil. The verb "overcome" (*nenikēkate*) is in the perfect tense, which indicates that the victory is already achieved but has continuing effects. Victory is not in the future. Victory has already happened in Jesus, and the young men who are fighting and struggling are doing so on the basis of a victory achieved. As John says later in the epistle, "You are from God, little children, and have overcome them; because greater is He who is in you than he who is in the world" (4:4).

Behind this triple division of the church is the Old Testament sequence of offices—priest, king, and prophet.[1] Priests are servants, who are given clear and detailed instructions for everything. They are "children," following rules and serving. Since the church is a priesthood, John can call *all* his readers "children." Kings have grown in maturity, and are called to make their own judgments about things as well as engage in battle. John's "young men" are kings. Prophets are sages, wise men who have their senses trained to discern between good and evil. They speak with authority because of that experience, and because of the Spirit in them, and so

---

1. See James Jordan, *From Bread to Wine*, available from Biblical Horizons, P.O. Box 1096, Niceville, florida, 32588.

they are "fathers" to the kings and direct the priests. Every church needs each of these. A church of priests is childish and potentially legalistic; a church of kings is potentially a church of hotheads; a church of fathers is too conservative to be healthy. Christ is priest, king, prophet in one, and a healthy body is a complex mix of priestly service, kingly battle, and prophetic sagacity.

THE WORLD

1 John 2:15Do not love the world or the things in the world. If anyone loves the world, the love of the Father is not in him. ¹⁶For all that is in the world—the desires of the flesh and the desires of the eyes and pride in possessions—is not from the Father but is from the world. ¹⁷And the world is passing away along with its desires, but whoever does the will of God abides forever.

The reference to overcoming the evil one links 2:12–14 with 2:15–17, which concentrates on the world. 2:15–17 is an intricately written exhortation, a Celtic knot of triads. The word "world" (*kosmon*) is used six times, "lust" (*epithumia*) and "love" (*agapaō* or *agapē*) three times each, and God is referred to three times as well, twice as Father and once as God.

John's theme is the division that runs down the human race. In John's view, creation—and the human race in particular—is divided into two. On the one side is the "family" of the church, the little children of the Father, consisting of those who are forgiven through Jesus, who have overcome the Evil One, and who are walking in the light. Opposed to the family of the church is "the world." Both in his letter and his gospel, John warns about "the world" (John 15–16; 1 John 2:15–17; 3:1, 13, 17; 4:1, 3–5, 9, 14, 17; 5:1, 4–5; 19). Christians are faithful to Jesus only when they resist the world.

We need to specify what John means both by "love" and "world." In some places, "world" refers to humanity or creation that is the object of God's love (John 3:16). In this sense, we are to share in the love of the Father for the world, which expresses itself in self-sacrifice for the salvation of the world. Jesus did not love the world in the sense of being seduced by it, or seeking to conform himself to it, or walking according to the pattern of the world. But he did love the world by seeking to save it. He loved the world by opposing it, challenging it, and ultimately giving himself for it. He loved the world so much that he died to transform it into something better.

"World" in 1 John 2 does not refer to humanity in this sense. Nor does it refer to the creation as such. When he condemns love of the world, John is not saying that we should despise creation. We should love daffodils and chipmunks and sunsets and waves on the ocean. Our love for the world should extend to cultural products as well. John doesn't condemn our love for Japanese gardens and the Taj Mahal and *Moby Dick* and the Goldberg Variations. Even pop culture is not specifically in his sights: we are not necessarily loving the world if we love Coca Cola and video games and *24* and U2. In themselves, all these things come from the hand of God, and are to be received with thanksgiving and joy.

Even these good things, of course, present subtle temptations. It's possible to love sunsets so much that we forget that they reveal only a small glimpse of the beauty of God. It is possible to get so caught up in the Brandenburg Concertos that we make an idol of music. This doesn't mean we have to think about God every moment of our lives. Nor does it mean that we love things only as vehicles and means for loving God. We should love the things he makes and gives us, love them for what they are, as the things they are, but we must always avoid turning them into ultimate goods. Faced with a choice between jazz and Jesus, there should be no question what has first place.

So, what *does* John mean by "world" in the statement "do not love the world"? In other places it refers specifically to humanity organized in its hostility to God (John 12:31; 14:30). Specifically, John has Judaism in mind, Judaism in its opposition to Jesus. That John uses the word "world" of Judaism is especially clear in John's gospel in chapters 15 and 16. Notice how John moves from talking about the disciples being hated and persecuted by "the world" to talking about "their law" and "the synagogues."

> If the world hates you, you know that it hated Me before it hated you. If you were of the world, the world would love its own. Yet because you are not of the world, but I chose you out of the world, therefore the world hates you. Remember the word that I said to you, 'A servant is not greater than his master.' If they persecuted Me, they will also persecute you. If they kept My word, they will keep yours also. But all these things they will do to you for My name's sake, because they do not know Him who sent Me. If I had not come and spoken to them, they would have no sin, but now they have no excuse for their sin. He who hates Me hates My Father also. If I had not done among them the works which no one else did, they would have no sin; but now they have seen and also hated both Me and My Father. But this happened that the word might be fulfilled which is written in their law, 'They hated Me without a cause.' These things I have spoken to you, that you should not be made to stumble. They will put you out of the synagogues; yes, the time is coming that whoever kills you will think that he offers God service. And these things they will do to you because they have not known the Father nor Me. But these things I have told you, that when the time comes, you may remember that I told you of them. (John 15:18–16:4)

Thus, the immediate context of the exhortation "Do not love the world" is this: first-century Christians were tempted to revert to Old Covenant patterns and standards, to maintain the divisions of Jew and Gentile that existed in the Old Covenant era, to adopt the fleshly ordinances of the Old Covenant. John says do not love this world, this world that is already passing away, this dark nighttime covenant that is already yielding to the dawn of the new covenant. This world, the first-century Jewish world, hates the Son, and therefore does not have the Father either. They do not have the gifts of God, but only corrupted forms of those gifts. The life of fleshly Israel is determined by flesh. It is not shaped by the desire for the gifts of God, but by perverse desire and by the false glory of boasting.

Judaism in its opposition to Jesus is the heart of what John calls "the world," but the world has a wider referent in the first century. At the time of Judah's exile, Yahweh set up a new world system, a series of Gentile empires, within which Israel was nestled.[2] That post-exilic *oikoumenē* was the world that was fading away in John's day (v. 17). When Jerusalem and its temple fell in 70 AD, that world came to an end. Rome continued, but Rome ceased to be the protective covering for Israel. By that time, Rome had turned from protector into attacker, as the beast from the sea, inspired by the land beast of Judaism, launched an assault on the saints. As the world of the post-exilic *oikoumenē* faded, the church was thrown into a world without protective imperial power. She had grown up, and was ready to leave home.

John's warnings, of course, continue to be relevant to us. By analogy, "world" refers to any religious, cultural, political, social, or economic system organized in opposition to God. God has continued to establish new "worlds" during the history of the New Covenant. The medieval world was religiously centered in Rome and politically fragmented into small principalities and duchies. Modernity reverses this arrangement: God has torn the church, so that there are many "centers" of Christian authority and inspiration, but massive bureaucratic political systems. At a smaller time scale, the political "world" of the twentieth century was a bi-polar world, split between the United States and the USSR. That world collapsed, and we are still trying to discern the contours of the world God is now forming.

By "world," John means these sorts of political and religious institutions, but he also has something more pervasive, intangible, subtle in mind—something we would be inclined to call "culture." For John, the *kosmon* that we renounce is a culture organized in opposition to, or indifference to, Jesus the Word of Life.

Modern political organization, for instance, arose in Europe in the aftermath of a series of vicious wars known (inaccurately) as

---

2. See James Jordan, *Handwriting on the Wall: A Commentary on the Book of Daniel* (Atlanta: American Vision, 2007).

"wars of religion." Though religion was only one factor in these wars, and not always the most important, most moderns believe the wars proved that public religion is deadly dangerous. If religion gets too close to power, it invariably turns fanatical and bloodthirsty. So early modern political theorists tried to devise political systems that could be run by anyone, regardless of creed or noncreed, and which did not depend on any shared religious faith. For centuries, this modern world wasn't overtly hostile to Christianity, and the church often flourished under the modern regime. After all, the vast majority of Europeans and Americans were Christians of one sort or another. In the last fifty years, however, religion has been ruled illegitimate in political life, and as a result we have a political system that, deliberately and in principle, treats God as if he were irrelevant to political life. We can worship freely, which is a wonderful blessing. We can believe whatever we want about God, or deny God altogether. We can even voice our opinions in public and try to urge a particular political agenda based on our theological beliefs. But if you're a politician, according to the Supreme Court, what you *cannot* do is to decide a piece of legislation on theological grounds. The American political system has become "world" in John's polemical sense. Not only does it systematically exclude Jesus, but it subtly tempts us to remove Jesus from our small mental box labeled "politics."

Economies can also be organized in ungodly ways. Many businesses today attempt to manipulate desires with advertising and marketing, hoping that we will become greedy or, at least, gripped with lust of the eyes and the pride of life. Economic systems can be arranged to protect large, corrupt, and inefficient mega-corporations and to keep new startup businesses from getting off the ground. Unions engage in thuggery to prevent a free labor market. American companies employ cheap overseas labor and keep workers in conditions that would be unconscionable in this country; but out of sight, out of mind. Overseas workers are often ecstatic to work for an American company, but the corporations frequently fail to treat them with the same dignity that they treat the better-organized workforce at home. Economic systems organized in defiance of God are part of the "world," and John warns us about these systems because they can penetrate our hearts, change our priorities, manipulate our desires.

Social systems are often organized in ways that are even closer to John's specific setting. One of the key features of the Judaism and Judaizing that John opposes was the division of humanity between Jew and Gentile. John, like Paul, insists that this binary division of humanity is passé, overcome in the cross and resurrection of Jesus. Judaizing is specifically an effort to erect social/religious boundaries where none should exist, between Jew and Gentile, between pure Jew and impure Jew, between holy and common. No such divisions should exist in a world where apostles see the Holy One in flesh, where they place their hands on the humanity of the Son of God. No such divisions exist once God has come out from behind the curtain and shown himself.

Yet modern societies often erect social barriers like those of Judaism. What is racism but another form of Judaizing, a reversion to the Old Covenant? What were Jim Crow laws but modernized versions of purity regulations? European aristocracies may not have treated lower classes as religious untouchables, but their practices very closely resemble traditional habits of impurity-avoidance. Unhappily, these worldly divisions have not been confined to the world outside the church. What is the division of Christian society into rigid social hierarchies, such as have existed many European societies, but a rending of Christ? A century ago, blacks and whites in the American South rarely sat together for worship, and even today Sunday morning is a segregated morning. Church growth experts Judaize when they plant churches for particular—usually upper middle-class—sectors of American socio-economic life. The social "world" tempts us to treat people according to its standards, and John warns us not to embrace those standards.

WORLD AND ITS LUSTS

I have been focusing on structural features of the "world," but John focuses attention on the relationship between the world and "desire." He enumerates three evil desires, or lusts (*epithumia*): the lust of the eyes, the lust of the flesh, and the boastful pride of life.

The desires John lists are, first of all, variations on the desires evoked by the tree of knowledge. Eve saw that the tree was good for food, a delight to the eyes, and desirable for wisdom (Gen. 3:6); she was gripped by the lust of the flesh, the lust of the eyes, and the boastful pride of life. Adam and Eve took the fruit of the tree of knowledge prematurely, but the things they desired from the tree were truly desirable, and God planned eventually to fulfill the desires of Eve's heart.

In the Old Covenant, Yahweh offered Israel the tree of knowledge in the form of three gifts, and then stored them away in the temple, hidden in the Most Holy Place, until the fullness of time, until Israel became mature enough to receive her inheritance. These are the three gifts in the ark: a jar of manna, the gift of food and life; the tablets of the law, written with the finger of God, the gift of instruction and wisdom; and the rod of Aaron that had budded with almond blossoms, the gift of authority, the gift of glory. Israel had these gifts in part: they had life in the presence of Yahweh, they had the wisdom of God in Torah, they had a share in the glory of God. But for Israel the fullness of these gifts lay in the future, and the life of each Israelite, and the life of Israel as a nation, was to be directed by desire for these three gifts, by the anticipation that someday the veil would be rent and the gifts would be opened and distributed freely. Yahweh promised that when he came forth from his tent, he would bring these gifts with him.

That is the gospel, which is, once again, the gospel of the rent veil. In the fullness of time, God sent these gifts not in part but in full. God sent Torah in the flesh, his Eternal Word and Wisdom; the Father sent bread from heaven, the One who is the way, the truth, and the *life*; he exalted humanity to heavenly places to share in his authority to judge. By his death and resurrection, Jesus tore down the veil where the gifts of God had been hidden away. By his death and resurrection, Jesus made these gifts available to anyone who trusts in him. Jesus *is* the life of God; Jesus *is* the Wisdom of God; Jesus *is* the glory of the Father, the exact representation and image of his Father. In Jesus, we have life and wisdom and royal glory. In Jesus, who is the ark of God, the gifts of God are freely offered to those who are united to Jesus and follow him. He is the tree of knowledge as he is the tree of life. Under the Old Covenant, these gifts were holy, taboo, unapproachable. But no longer; now, it's holy things for the holy people.

Our lives as individuals, and as a community of believers, are to be shaped by these gifts, and by our desire for these gifts. To live as a Christian is to have our love directed to Jesus, who is the way, truth, life, who is the wisdom of God, who is the glory of God. To live as a Christian community is to be formed and shaped by the love of Jesus, by the desire for the life, wisdom, and glory that the Father gives through him and his Spirit.

Already in Israel's history, however, the Jews had begun to direct their loves and desires elsewhere. Instead of seeking the glory that comes from God, Jesus and Paul accused Jews of seeking praise from man (Matt. 23:6; John 5:44; Rom. 2:29); their lives became directed by the pride of life, pride in their own works, boastfulness in their own status as members of God's covenant people. Instead of seeking the wisdom of God's commandments, they began to create their own commandments, exchanging the word of God for their own laws; they did not love and desire the Lord's wisdom, but instead lusted after something that they believed was desirable to the eyes and able to make them wise. Some, such as Philo, were tempted to receive the wisdom of the Greeks, and so they indulged the lust of the eyes. Instead of receiving the life that God offered them through his Spirit and his food, they sought the life of the flesh, gloried in their descent from Abraham and in circumcision. Instead of being shaped and formed by their desire for God and his gifts, they became distorted and misshapen: they did not love God's life, wisdom, and glory; they sought life elsewhere, relied on their own wisdom, enhanced out their own glory. These are the evil desires that John has in mind.

As John presents it, though, the relationship between the world and desire is complex. On the one hand, the world *consists of* desires and boasting. Verse 16 indicates that desires and boastfulness make up the contents of the world—the desire of flesh, eyes, and boastful-ness of life constitute the "all that is in the world" (*pan to en tō kosmō*). The end of verse 16, however, suggests that the world is the *source* of desires and boasts: the desire of flesh, desire of eyes, and boastful-ness of life are *from* the world (*ek tou kosmou*). Desires make up the world, yet the world also produces, evokes, provokes desires and boastfulness. On the other hand, desire is also the guiding principle of the world. Verse 17 distinguishes between the world and its de-sires as if the desires are accompaniments of the world. So, the world as John is describing it is a *product* of desires and boasting, and also *encourages* desires and boasting. Desires are the "contents" of cul-ture—culture is made up of embodied dreams, aspirations, lusts; on the other hand, culture embodies desire; on yet another hand, the world is the source of desire, evoking certain kinds of desire.

John's suggestion that the world is made up not only of "things" (*ta en tō kosmō*, v. 15) but also of "desires" yields rich insights into Christian living. He does not limit the "world" to the artifacts of the world, nor to the institutions and practices of the world. At its heart, the world is a collection of desires. To put it more sociologically, (sin-ful) human culture—its institutions, practices, products—are all ex-ternalizations of evil desire or boastfulness. John thus hints that we should evaluate the world not only on the basis of what is done or what things it contains, but on the basis of desire.

Much Christian cultural criticism concentrates on the obvious, superficial annoyances and evils of modern life. Abortion, homo-sexuality, the expulsion of God from public life—these are evident evils and Christians have rightly taken their stand against these. John encourages us to penetrate below the surface of cultural life to the desires that are provoking, and are provoked by, the world. John's cultural criticism encourages us to ask what desires are em-bodied in the products of human labor—in roads, skyscrapers, automobiles, iPods, coffee, customs, schools, and so on.

What desires, for example, lie behind the revolution in infor-mation technologies? You might say the desire to make communi-cation more efficient, to distribute information faster and more widely. At least some in the information tech industries have

higher aspirations: they hope to create a new human race—
disembodied, incorporeal, above all, networked. They aim at a kind
of godlike transcendence of limits of body and place, time and
space, a gnostic escape from creaturehood. Max More, a leading
"Extropian," a group dedicated to investigating how human beings
can overcome the problem of entropy, says that through various
practices and technologies, we can aim at "the removal of political,
cultural, biological limits to self-actualization and self-realization."
More says, "Shrugging off the limits imposed on us by our natural
heritage, we apply the evolutionary gift of our rational, empirical
intelligence to surpass the confines of our humanity, crossing the
threshold into the transhuman and posthuman stages that await
us." Posthumanity is achievable through technology: "When technology allows us to reconstitute ourselves physically, genetically,
and neurologically, we who have become transhuman will be
primed to transform ourselves into posthumans—persons of un-
precedented physical, intellectual and psychological capacity, self-
programming, potentially immortal, unlimited individuals."[3]

What desires, what kind of boasting, lie behind the giant slide
that for a few months occupied the main gallery in London's Tate
Modern? What desire was the "artist" trying to fulfill by setting up
a slide in one of the world's foremost art museums? If he's looking
for fame, he got it; the slide was reported on NPR. Can an artist get
any more famous than that? If he desires to challenge conceptions
of what makes art, art, to transgress boundaries between art and
play, he got that done, too.

When you evaluate an artifact, or a fashion, or a trend in culture, ask what desires and what pride motivate the designer, the
inventor, the artist. This doesn't determine whether we are free to
use these products. Information technologies might be invented by
people who want to become eternal minds, but that doesn't mean
that everyone who uses these technologies has the same desires.

3. Erik Davis, *Techgnosis: Myth, Magic, and the Mysticism of the Age of Information* (five Star, 2005), 143–45.

The wealth of the wicked is stored up for the righteous; Cain built the first city, but the final order of things will also be a city, the city of God (Gen. 4:20–22). Everything is clean for us. But if we want to understand where our culture has come from and is going, we must discern the desires that give it life.

Equally important is the other side of this culture-desire link. The desire or boasting that motivated the creators does not determine whether we use these things. Desires and boasting that are evoked by the world are more determinative. We must ask not only what desires are incarnated in cultural artifacts and practices, but also how *my* desires are being shaped, distorted, or refreshed by the things I view, and use, and play with.

There are obvious examples of entertainments that shape our desires in sinful ways: pornographic films, web sites, ads that either elicit sexual desire directly, or use the aura of sexual desire to make something else desirable. Sex is so tantalizing that a sexy ad can create the illusion that Miller Beer is actually beer. Desire for sex not only drives much of entertainment and marketing, but is behind the development of contraceptives, the massive and lucrative institutions of the abortion industry, educational policies, and so on. Desire for free, uninhibited, unconstrained sex is one of the main driving forces of our culture, and this desire has been embodied in countless institutions, practices, and artifacts.

Christians know they have to resist sexual lust. Most of the challenges we face are not, however, so easy and obvious. We know that we should avoid pornography because it is so overt and, as it were, honest about the desires it evokes. What about advertisements that don't play the sex card? What about advertisements that play the comfort-and-luxury card? What about advertisements that evoke a desire for a particular kind of lifestyle, a particular level of income? What about ads that encourage me to think of myself as the center of the universe, the cosmic cat that all other created things were made to serve? We immediately put up our defenses when we see a pornographic image, but what about an ad that evokes greed? Are we as quick to turn away and reject it? What about a song that encourages autonomy, that strokes pride, one that encourages you to act by your own wisdom and not to seek out the wisdom of others? What about a technology that flatters you with the sense that you are the center of the universe? What about a film that encourages you to think that wrongs should be corrected by vengeance and violence, films that encourage you to think people are cool when they take the law into their own hands?

Even cultural products that are good or innocuous in themselves can shape our desires in perverse directions. Communications technologies affect the way we experience communication and inter-personal relations, transform expectations about time, and might encourage impatience and a desire for instant results. Cars are a great blessing, but think of the way the invention of the automobile permitted us, and particularly young people, a freedom we had never had. Technologies make new things possible, but we need to ask whether all the new things made possible are things we should desire.

This is not a question of high culture versus popular culture. High culture is not necessarily godly, and popular culture not necessary ungodly. Ask yourself when you listen to Bartok, what are the desires, what is the boasting, that leads to this? Ask yourself when you pick out a film or watch your favorite television show, or sit down to play a video game, or decide whether or not to purchase an iPhone: Why do I want this? Why do I want to listen to this particular song? What kinds of desires is it awakening? Don't confine your examination to the message. We think we can protect ourselves by evaluating the worldview of a particular book or film. We watch a movie, see that it encourages vengeance, violence, or greed, and we say that we have not been influenced by it. We conclude that we're safe, but we're kidding ourselves: films, music, games, TV shows are shaping us in far more subtle ways, evoking desires that are not captured by rejecting the "message."

Ask yourself whether those desires are the kinds of desires that the Bible encourages. Paul says that we should think on, meditate on, desire things that are lovely, true, honorable, right, and excellent. Our desires should be desire for fellowship with God in Christ, hunger and thirst for righteousness, desire to grow in wisdom and maturity, desire for the praise that comes from God. Before you pick up the next video or CD, before you choose how you're going to spend Friday evening, ask whether the choice encourages these desires or the desires that come from the world.

Above all, don't try to sidestep John's exhortation. John says, "Do not love the world or the things in the world," and we immediately scurry around to find rationalizations and escape routes. Is John saying that cigarettes and beer and symphony orchestras and dancing and watching movies and art museums and playing video games are inherently sinful? Didn't God himself love the world enough to send his own Son to die for it? We don't want to retreat from engagement with the culture and political life around us. We don't want to be Gnostics. We don't want to be Mennonites, Pietists, or prairie muffins.

When we're honest, we recognize that these objections and rationalizations often—not always—reduce to a single fundamental objection: we don't want to be uncool. We don't want to stand out and look odd. We want to do whatever feels good, whatever makes us happy, whatever keeps us well within the boundaries of the mainstream of the world. Yet that's precisely the attitude that John tells us to avoid. We have often flirted with the world, conforming to its expectations, instead of living with steady devotion to the Father. flirtation is precisely the right word for it: James says, "You adulteresses, do you not know that friendship with the world is hostility to God? Therefore whoever wishes to be a friend of the world makes himself an enemy of God" (4:4).

Against all our rationalizations and justifications and flirtations, John's warning is stark: do not love the world. He adds that those who do love the world don't have the love of the Father. He poses an either/or: your love can be oriented in one of two directions, toward the Father or toward the world. There is no third way. Of course, we must determine what John means by "world," but at the outset we must vigorously resist the temptation to define John's warning out of existence. We must resist the temptation to turn "do not love the world" into "do it your way."

6

ANTICHRIST AND THE ANOINTING
1 John 2:18–29

In a 1999 article, Jeffrey Goldberg of *Slate* and the *New York Times* described an encounter with the late Jerry Falwell.

> Early one shiny autumn morning, I got in my car and drove to Lynchburg, Va., in order to find out whether or not I am the Antichrist. You know: the Beast, the Worthless Shepherd, the Little Horn, the Abomination, the linchpin of the Diabolical Trinity.
>
> That Antichrist.
>
> I had my suspicions. Nowhere on my body could I find the mark of the Beast—666—but I do have a freckle that's shaped like Bermuda. And though I have never been seized by a desire to lead the armies of Satan in a final, bloody confrontation with the forces of God on the plain of Armageddon, I do suffer from aggravated dyspepsia, as well as chronic malaise, conditions that I'm sure afflict the Antichrist.

The surest suspicion I had about my pivotal role in Christian eschatology grew from the fact that I am Jewish, male, and alive. These are the qualifications for the job of Antichrist as specified by Lynchburg's most famous preacher, Jerry Falwell, in a speech he made earlier this year.

Later in the article, he asks Falwell if he might be the Antichrist.

Falwell chuckled a condescending chuckle. "It's almost amusing, that question. Of course not. I know that you're not."

Why?

"The Antichrist will be a world leader, he'll have supernatural powers," he said.
He got me there—I have no supernatural powers. I can't even drive a stick shift.[1]

Christians have speculated about the identity of the antichrist for centuries. Normally, the procedure conflates the "antichrist" in John's letters to one of the "beasts" in Revelation 13. The resulting compound is a single person known as Antichrist who gains absolute political power and persecutes believers and who will appear on the stage of human history sometime in the future, usually the near future.

Medieval commentator Adso of Montier-en-Der wrote a treatise on the anti-Christ, and throughout the Middle Ages popes and emperors traded the insult. The Reformers sometimes identified the papacy itself as Antichrist. In more recent decades, Henry Kissinger has been an erstwhile favorite for the role. By using the numbers attached to Hebrew letters, and by spelling George Bush's name in Hebrew, we learn that his name adds up to 666. There's a sticking point, though: the beast has seven heads, and we have no

---

1. Goldberg, "I, Antichrist?" *Slate* (November 5, 1999), available at http://www.slate.com/id/45483, accessed December 23, 2008.

evidence that Bush has more than one (and many wonder about the existence even of that). Ahh, but: according to one web site,

> [t]hese seven master empires in chronological order are Babylon (both Old and New), Egypt, Assyria, Medo-Persia, Greece or Macedonia, Rome, and finally the United States. Of course, this doesn't include the Chinese, Inca, Mayan etc., because they were either unknown or too far removed from the Biblical world, which includes the Mediterranean world of the Middle East and Europe. This remains the critical heart of the Biblical world, even today. It doesn't include empires like the British and Ottoman because their power was actively contested by contemporaries, and they never held the sort of "sole superpower" status that once marked Rome, and currently defines the USA.[2]

You know that horn thing that Bush does with his fingers? He claims it's the Texas Longhorn symbol, but those who know say it's the international sign of Satan worship.

Nero and the Pope and Peter the Great and Hitler and Osama bin Laden and Saddam Hussein and John F. Kennedy and Prince Charles and Ronald Reagan and any of a hundred other historical figures have been identified as antichrist. It is all ludicrous, and makes Christians look ridiculous.

FIRST-CENTURY ANTICHRIST

1 John 2:18 Children, it is the last hour, and as you have heard that antichrist is coming, so now many antichrists have come. Therefore we know that it is the last hour. [19]They went out from us, but they were not of us; for if they had been of us, they would have continued with us. But they went out, that it might become plain that they all are not of us. [20]But you have been anointed by the Holy One, and you all have knowledge. [21]I write to you, not be-

---

2. "George Walker Bush Is the Antichrist," available at http://thebirdman.org/Index/Others/Others-Doc-Religion&Spirituality/+Doc-Religion&Spirituality-ReligiousEvil&Strangeness/GeorgeWBush IsTheAntichrist.htm, accessed December 23, 2008.

cause you do not know the truth, but because you know it, and because no lie is of the truth. ²²Who is the liar but he who denies that Jesus is the Christ? This is the antichrist, he who denies the Father and the Son. ²³No one who denies the Son has the Father. Whoever confesses the Son has the Father also. ²⁴Let what you heard from the beginning abide in you. If what you heard from the beginning abides in you, then you too will abide in the Son and in the Father. ²⁵And this is the promise that he made to us—eternal life.

John would have found it ridiculous too. He tells us pretty clearly what he's talking about. First, he says that it's the last hour (2:18), and he does not mean that the "last hour" is *always* close to us. God doesn't play with time like that. He created the world in six days and told us so, and the Bible is packed with accurate chronological information. God does not sniff with gnostic indifference at calendars and temporal calculations. When John says "last hour" he means *last hour*. Something is nearing the end. As I have noted above, we have two choices: either John was wrong or he was referring to the end of something other than the space-time universe.

Evangelicals frequently insist that Jesus is coming soon. For some, this almost functions as a test case of evangelical eschatology. If you believe the Bible, and take it "literally," then you will say that Jesus is coming soon, but this does not fit the biblical picture, and it does not reflect a very literal reading of Scripture. If Jesus returns tomorrow, I will be proven wrong, and happily so, but I am convinced that Jesus will not return for many millennia. The great Princeton theologian B. B. Warfield said in the last century the church was still living in its infancy. We are still living in the early days of the church, and have millennia of maturation left. That fits what I think the Bible teaches. Let me explain a bit.

The New Testament teaches that Christ is coming "soon," but the New Testament was written two thousand years ago, and the parousia spoken of by the apostles was imminent for *that* generation. The apostles were not mistaken, and the only "delay of the parousia" was a delay of years or decades. These prophecies were fulfilled in the events surrounding the fall of Jerusalem in 70 AD.

Besides, many of the biblical descriptions of the future kingdom seem to assume a lengthy period of growth—time for the seed to grow into the largest tree of the field (Matt. 13), for the stone to grow into a mountain that fills the earth (Dan. 2), for the earth to become filled with the knowledge of the Lord as the waters cover the sea (Isa. 11). Before he returns, the Lord will take the time to bring blessing on "thousands of generations" of those who love him and keep his commandments (Ex. 20:5–6).

Finally, and drawing not from specific texts but rather from the penumbra of Scripture, it would seem odd if the Lord gave Adam a commission to rule and subdue the earth, sent his Son to die and rise again as the Last Adam to restore humanity to that task, and then ended the whole process after a couple thousand years, just when we were beginning to make a few meager advances in our dominion over creation. Humanity—I say it with reverence—would feel more than a little cheated, like a teenager never given a chance to grow up. Most editions of the *Book of Common Prayer* include a table for calculating the dates for feast days, and the table can be used up to about the year 6000 AD. I'm with those guys, except that I think the Prayer Book will need a much more extended table before all is said and done.

"Antichrist" is one of the themes of the last part of 1 John 2, but it is woven into a number of other themes. Verse 18 begins a new section, with John addressing his readers directly as "children" (*paidia*) and bringing up the "last hour" for the first time in the letter. Verses 18–29 form a neatly ordered section:

A. Children, antichrists coming, they went out, 2:18–19
  B. You have an anointing, knowledge, 2:20
    C. I have written, truth/lie, 2:21
      D. Antichrist is liar, denies Son and Father, 2:22
        E. Deny Son, deny Father, 2:23
      D′ Abide in what you have, abide in Father and Son, 2:24–25
    C′ I have written, those who deceive, 2:26
  B′ You have an anointing, knowledge, 2:27
A′ Little children (*teknia*), Christ coming; abide, 2:28–29

This structure clarifies a number of things in the passage. The "last hour" of verse 18 matches the warning about the Lord's "coming" in 2:28, so the "last hour" means the "last hour" before the parousia of Jesus. The structure also underscores the fact that Jesus is going to deal with the antichrists. John starts by warning about the antichrists, but at the end assures his readers that Jesus is coming—like the world Emperor he is—to scatter his enemies and rescue his people. This fits the first-century situation perfectly: John's churches are seduced and oppressed by Judaizing heretics, and Jesus is coming within the hour to tear down their last fortress, the temple in Jerusalem.

What marks the antichrists is the fact that they do not "remain" (*menō*) with "us" (v. 19). John returns to this theme at the end of the section, assuring his readers that the anointing "abides" (*menō*, v. 27) in them and urging them to abide in him, presumably Christ, in preparation for his coming. Finally, verses 20 and 27 (two times) are the only two places in the New Testament where the word "anointing" (*chrisma*) is used. This triple repetition of the word fits with John's preference for triads, and also probably points to a trinitarian dimension of the anointing.

In fact, this whole passage is suffused with trinitarian references. Antichrists are defined as those who "deny that Jesus is the Christ" (v. 22), and John goes on to insist that denying the Son entails denying the Father also. The Son is the revelation of the Father, the "Way" to the Father (John 15). Anyone who rejects the Son effectively rejects the Father whose image the Son is. Abiding in the Son, by contrast, means also abiding in the Father (v. 24). In this context, John talks about the anointing, a reference, I shall argue below, to the Holy Spirit. The Spirit is the one who gives knowledge (v. 20) by abiding in those who receive him and follow Jesus (v. 27). John's readers are among those incorporated into the Triune fellowship, while antichrists, by rejecting Jesus, have shut themselves off from the only path to that fellowship. Again we can refer back to the opening message of the letter: the Triune God has shown himself, and brought his people near into intimate fellowship, a fellowship possible only because the Lord has come into our world in tangible, visible flesh.

This structure also helps us to see how John defines the "antichrist." John is clearly not talking about a single individual because he uses the word in the plural (2:18). And he helpfully defines what he means by "antichrist": the "one who denies that Jesus is the Christ," which also means "the one who denies the Father and the Son" (2:22; cf. 2 John 7). We need to read verses 18 and 19 in the light of verses 22 and 23, the central section of the chiasm, in order to understand what John means by "antichrists."

GOING FROM US

John writes that his readers are living in the last hours of the old world, the world of the Old Covenant and the *oikoumenē*, and he knows what time it is because Jesus' predictions about false prophets and false christs are coming to pass (cf. Matt. 24:22–24; cf. 1 John 4:1). Jesus not only predicted the rise of false christs, but also the beginning of an apostasy (Matt. 24:11–12), and John appears to mention the same phenomenon in two interwoven chiasms of verse 19:

> Out of us (*ex hēmōn*)
> > they went out (*exēlthan*)
> > > but not
> > they were (*ēsan*)
> out of us (*ex hēmōn*).

> if out of us (*ex hēmōn*)
> > were (*ēsan*)
> > they had remained
> with us (*meth' hēmōn*).

John uses the phrase "from us" or "out of us" in two senses: in the first sense, the antichrists have gone out "from us," but in the second sense they were never "from us." It appears that the antichrists are "from us" in the sense that the "us" is the starting point for a journey. But they *are* not from us: "being from us" does not describe the character of the antichrists, though it describes their place of departure. If we take this as a general statement about the apostasy of the antichrists, the meaning is: "They left us, but they did not belong to us. If they had truly belonged to us, they would have stayed with us." Alternatively, John may not be talking about apostasy in general, but instead about unauthorized missionaries. In that case, the meaning is: "Geographically, they started out from us, but we didn't send them—we did not commission them. If they had been commissioned, they would have continued to associate with us and to share in our confession of Jesus as the Christ."

The latter interpretation is preferable for several reasons. First, the "us" of verse 19 is probably not "us believers" but "us apostles." That is how John uses the first person plural at the beginning of his letter, distinguishing between the apostolic "us" and the "you" that receives the apostolic witness (1:1–4). He makes the same distinction between first and second person here: "They went from *us* . . . but *you* have an anointing . . . *I* have not written to *you*." Second, the chiastic structure of the letter assists us as well. As noted in chapter 2, 2:18–29 parallels 4:1–6; both refer to an antichrist coming, and both mention the Spirit (2:20 calls the Spirit the "anointing," while 4:1–6 explicitly speaks of the "Spirit of truth"). In 4:5–6, John distinguishes between the antichrists and "us." Antichrists are from the world (*ek tou kosmou*) but "*we* are from God" (*ek tou theou*). Antichrists have an audience with the world (v. 5), while the one who knows God listens to "us." John is not making a statement about the church in general, but about the apostles: listening to the *apostles* is the test of whether one is filled with the Spirit of truth or the spirit of error. Since the first person plural refers to the apostles in 4:1–6, it most likely does in 2:19.

We can reconstruct the background to 2:19 as follows: when persecution broke out in Jerusalem following the martyrdom of Stephen, believers fled from the city, leaving only the apostles behind (Acts 8:2). After Paul and Barnabas began to have success among Gentiles, startled Jews from Judea and Jerusalem spread out to the churches, urging Gentiles to Judaize—to receive circumcision and observe Torah (Acts 15:1; Gal. 2:11–12). Though they confessed

Jesus in some sense, they did not believe that Jesus broke the dividing wall of Jew and Gentile and brought in a new and better covenant. They did not believe that Jesus brought an end to the world of restriction, taboo, purity, and avoidance. In effect, they denied that Jesus is the Messiah (1 John 2:22). While the Judaizers went out "from us," that is, from Jerusalem, they were not really "from us"—from the apostles—but from the world. Had they been from the apostles, they would have remained in fellowship with them, and would have preached the same gospel. Instead, they stopped listening to the apostles and began preaching and listening to "the world" (4:5), that is, the old world of Judaism. Their independence from the apostles manifests that they were not "of us."

Though John is not talking about apostasy per se, the Judaizing false teachers are in fact apostates. They started out with the apostles, and confessed Jesus, but they rapidly went in a different direction. Apostasy raises problems for some believers, especially for Reformed believers. The P in TULIP refers to the perseverance of the saints, which is sometimes taken to mean that apostasy is not possible. Once we pray the prayer or experience salvation, we are in for good, no matter what. That is not, however, what "perseverance" means in the Reformed tradition. It does not mean that once we have had some experience of salvation or professed faith or been regenerated, we are free to sit back on our laurels and just slide along. It means that God preserves his people through all temptations and difficulties and backslidings. Those whom God loved and chose before the foundation of the world will in fact continue in faith because of the mercy of God. It also means that God will preserve his church, and will never remove the lampstand.

Yet the promise of assistance to the end coexists with the danger of apostasy. Some receive all sorts of blessings in the New Covenant—tasting the powers of the age to come, participating in the Spirit, being enlightened by the gift of the Spirit, being cleansed from the defilements of the world, but then fall away (Heb. 6:4–6). For a time, they share in blessings of salvation. John makes it clear that the sign of true faith is "remaining with us." When apostates "go out," that is the signal that whatever they experienced of Jesus and his Spirit, they do not have an eternal share in Christ.

According to John, these do not merely "go out" but also begin to spread false teaching. Again, the structure highlights this connection. In verse 21, he states that he writes to people who already know the truth, but the corresponding verse 26 indicates that he needs to confirm them in the truth because some are "trying to deceive you." In context, those who are trying to deceive are the antichrists who have gone away from the apostolic community. This point again supports the second interpretation of verse 19 mentioned above, namely, that those "who went out" were not apostates in general but specifically teachers whose mission did not bear an apostolic imprimatur. This is not just a formality. Just as Jesus says to false teachers "I never knew you" (Matt. 7:13–23), so John says that the false missionaries were never "of us" (v. 19). He is not merely saying that these false teachers lacked formal approval, but they were not fully with the apostles to begin with.

For John's readers, antichrists are people from within the church who leave and abandon the apostles, and who now oppose the church by embarking on a vigorous mission of teaching falsehood, denying the Christ who bought them. This describes the Judaizers quite accurately.

Does that mean we don't have to worry about antichrists anymore? Not at all. Anyone who denies that Jesus is the Christ, or denies that the Son of God came in the flesh is antichrist—against Christ. And we have plenty of these around. Some are overtly opposed to Jesus, such as cults that describe Jesus as a great man or the highest of the creatures. In the modern world there have also been many within the mainstream of the church who have questioned what John says is the *sine qua non* of Christian faith—the confession that Jesus is the Christ. They have reduced Jesus to a great moral teacher, a good man, a revolutionary leader. They do not think that he is God in human flesh. These false teachers have seduced many into false teaching, and turned many away from the gospel.

Apostasy is still possible too. How do we have confidence we will persevere? How can we know that God will preserve us?

John's readers escape the deceptions of antichrists if they remain (*menō*) in the things they heard from John and the other apostles (2:24). If we persevere, it is not because we are better than those who drift or run away. It is not that God gets us started and then we run on our own steam after that. The Christian life is a life of faith from first to last, from beginning to end. Perseverance is perseverance in *faith*. So, trust God. This trust takes form in particular practices. God preserves us, but God uses means to preserve us. One of those means is the message of the gospel itself. The phrase "from the beginning" (v. 24) reminds us of the opening verses of John's letter, where John describes the things that the apostles have known from the beginning — essentially, the story of Jesus, his life and his teaching. The way to escape the deception of antichrists is to continue to believe and remember the message heard from the beginning, along with the way of life that this message implies. Go back to the gospel, to the life and ministry of Jesus.

ANOINTING

^{1 John 2:26}I write these things to you about those who are trying to deceive you. ²⁷But the anointing that you received from him abides in you, and you have no need that anyone should teach you. But as his anointing teaches you about everything, and is true, and is no lie — just as it has taught you, abide in him.

John is confident that his readers will be preserved from the error of false teachers not only because of the message they heard, and their efforts to remember it, but also because of God's promise. His confidence is ultimately in God and the "anointing" that believers have received.

A pun in the Greek supports this point. The false teachers are called "antichrists" (*antichristoi*), and the protection from these antichrists comes from the "anointing" (*chrisma*, v. 27). They continue to abide in the Christ, the Anointed One, by sharing in his anointing. Verse 27 is neatly organized:

A. You received anointing
   B. It remains in you
      C. You have no need that one teach you
A' But anointing teaches you concerning all things
         D. And is true, not a lie
      C' Just as it teaches
   B' Remain in him

The repetition of the verb "remain" (*menō*) links the B sections, but there is an inversion. In B, the anointing "remains in you." The believer is the "home" in which the anointing finds residence. At the end of the verse, however, John exhorts his readers to "abide in Him." Dweller and dwelling change places, and the two clauses together point to a perichoretic relationship between the anointing, Christ, and the believer. We are temples of the Spirit, dwelling places for God, and at the same time Christ is our dwelling place, our home, our living temple.

What does it mean for believers to share in the anointing? In the Old Testament, priests and kings were anointed, and John is implying that his readers, because they are in Christ the Anointed, are all priests and kings (cf. Rev. 1:6; 5:10). But the specific referent for the anointing seems to be the Holy Spirit, who is commonly associated with anointings. When Samuel anoints David with oil, the Spirit comes on him to equip him for war and to enable him to be a faithful king (1 Sam. 16:13). The messiah in Isaiah describes himself as one anointed with the Spirit, and Jesus applies these words to himself in his first sermon in Nazareth (Isa. 61:1; Luke 4:18; Acts 10:38). Concretely, the anointing refers to the gift of the Spirit, who has been poured out on the church and who leads the church into truth (John 16:13; 1 Cor. 2:10). Because the members of the church are anointed with the Spirit, they know the truth. To combat deceivers, antichrists, and false prophets, they must continue in the Spirit that anointed them (2:27).

John's reference to anointing fits with the major themes of the gospel as he proclaims it in the letter. He says explicitly that the anointing comes "from the Holy" (*ek tou hagiou*), which could refer to a person (the "Holy One") or to a place. The ambiguity is probably deliberate. Christians receive an anointing from the Holy One of Israel, and the anointing itself is the Holy Spirit, but that anointing is also flowing from the now-opened Holy Place of the temple. Anointed "from the Holy," Christians are themselves holy. The indwelling presence of the Spirit is another sign that the gospel proclaims the end of ancient religious order, with its sharp distinctions between holy and profane and its rules of purity. Every believer, not just some temple elite, *knows* because every believer has received a holy unction from the Holy.

John could be referring to an actual anointing with oil. Anointings occur in the Old Testament, and many churches have continued to anoint at either baptism or confirmation. In the New Testament, rites of anointing are done mainly for healing (cf. Jas. 5:13–18), and there is no indication that an anointing accompanied the water of baptism. Instead, the New Testament bundles together the various initiation rites of the Old Testament—circumcision, royal or priestly anointing, investiture, washing—into the single rite of water baptism. "Anointing" describes part of the meaning and reality of baptism, but does not prescribe a part of the rite. John 2:20 does contribute to baptismal theology, however, by highlighting the fact that all believers share in the anointing of Jesus, all are holy with the anointing "from the Holy," all are priests and kings, all have access to the holy things and places, and all share in the life of the Spirit who animates the body of the Son.

As important as teaching and instruction are, as important as creeds and confessions are, as important as doctrine is, our perseverance and assurance of remaining with God, and our assurance that we will not be seduced by false teaching, does not lie in anything we do, any security we achieve, any document or structure or institution. It lies in *God*, in the work that the Spirit is doing in us, in the assurance that the God who began a good thing will complete it. Persevering faith is continuing trust and confidence in the historical work of Jesus—what we heard from the beginning. And persevering faith is trusting that the Anointing of the Spirit is at work in us, and relying on that Spirit to complete the work he began. Trusting the

Spirit for salvation does not undermine trust in Christ, because the Spirit is Christ's Spirit, and Paul goes so far as to say that the "Lord [Jesus] is the Spirit" (2 Cor. 3:17). Perseverance is perseverance in the anointing promised and given in baptism; perseverance is what the Westminster larger catechism calls improving on baptism.

"You have no need for anyone to teach you," John writes, since "His anointing teaches you about all things" (2:27). Whatever this means, it certainly does not mean that Christians do not need any teachers. That would make John's statement contradictory, since he would be teaching his readers they do not need teachers (except *him*, apparently). Besides, the New Testament makes it clear that teachers are essential to the church. Paul mentions teaching as a gift of the *Spirit*, and in Ephesians he reiterates that when Christ ascended he gave teachers to the church, as well as apostles, prophets, and evangelists (Eph. 4:11–12).

Christians have sometimes taken John's statement out of this context and concluded they don't need any human guidance or instruction. Even Christians who don't renounce teachers in principle often act as if they don't need any help, as if they can survive and flourish in the Christian life without instruction from anyone. The rebellious child who refuses to listen to his parents; the husband who won't take counsel about how to deal with a troubled marriage; the young man with credit card debt who keeps trying to solve the problem without getting help: refusal to hear instruction is not a sign of spirituality but a sign of arrogance, and a sure prescription for failure. Teachers are God's gift to the church; we can't prosper if we are contemptuous of God's gifts.

The Spirit is the ultimate teacher who leads us into all truth, and there are certainly times when the Spirit speaks through teachers who are outside the mainstream of the church. Luther was one such teacher, a mouthpiece of the Spirit who blows where he lists. Even when the Spirit speaks outside normal channels, he still works through men. God has determined to proclaim his gospel through men, both to humble us and to teach us what it means to love one another. Refusing to listen to the teachers whom the Lord gives is not spirituality. It is the opposite of spirituality because it grieves the Spirit.

HIS COMING

Verse 28 has often been taken as a reference to the final judgment, when we will all have to stand before the Lord, but the word "coming" or "appearance" (parousia) can also refer to a coming or an appearance of Jesus in history. The Greek word is used in royal and imperial ideology and practice to refer to the arrival of the emperor or king. When a king arrives in a conquered city, the citizens stand for inspection. Those who have been rebelling against him may be executed, while those who have remained faithful to him are rewarded and elevated. The first parousia occurred in Eden, when the Lord came in the Spirit of the Day to confront Adam with his sin. Adam did not stand up well. He shrank back in shame because he had succumbed to the temptation of the devil and had listened to the lies of antichrist. John does not want the same to happen to his readers: when Jesus appears, he wants his readers to have confidence, and not slink back in shame before Jesus.

Structurally, as noted above, the appearance is God's response to the false teachers and antichrists, who have come in the "last hour." Jesus is going to appear, and this means there is going to be a massive crisis soon. It is the last hour before his arrival, and the king is about to come. When he does, some will be destroyed—the antichrists in particular—and others will be commended. Employing a pun in Greek (v. 28), John exhorts his readers to abide in Christ so that they will have confidence (*parrēsian*) at his coming (*parousia*).

To stand when the Son arrives, John's readers need to be persevering in faith *and* in righteous obedience. Remaining in the Son and abiding in the anointing of the Spirit is not a mystical experience. It certainly is mysterious, and our relationship with the Spirit always has some kind of mystical dimensions. Abiding is fundamentally about living day to day as a Christian, obeying the commandments of Jesus. That is John's theme at the end of chapter 2:

having brought up the prospect of Jesus' appearance and the coming inspection, he tells his readers they need to practice righteousness (v. 29). This is a striking maneuver. When discussions of judgment come up, many Protestants think immediately of the imputed righteousness of Jesus. We only have confidence when Jesus comes because we stand in his righteousness, not our own. John's mind moves differently. He does emphasize that we are in Christ and abide in him, but when he talks about righteousness that stands in the judgment he is talking about *practiced* righteousness, righteousness-in-action, the "one who *does* righteousness" (*ho poiōn tēn dikaiosunēn*, v. 29). This righteousness is a gift as much as imputed righteousness is. It is from God's free grace. Yet, we have confidence at the Lord's appearance because the anointing that abides in us has produced a life of righteousness. Trusting in the work of the Spirit, we live lives of obedience. The one who is righteous by faith lives at the judgment, and beyond.

7

PRACTICING RIGHTEOUSNESS
1 John 2:28–3:24

Everyone can see that the human race is divided. There are some dozens of wars going on in the world at the moment, and even where there is no war, nations and tribes and clans battle one another. The world is divided by race, by national boundaries, by blood and soil, by economic or social class, by age, by cultural tastes. Scripture acknowledges a fundamental division in the human race, but the division is not national or racial, social or economic or cultural. The main division is between two families who descend from two fathers.

This is what Yahweh told Adam and Eve to expect when he appeared to them in the garden after they had sinned (Gen. 3:15). There would be enmity between the seed of the woman and the seed of the serpent. Adam and Eve were no sooner driven from the Garden than warfare manifested itself in Cain's murder of Abel.

Over the following centuries, the descendants of Seth and the descendants of Cain ran in separate lines and were sometimes hostile toward one another.

That history of warfare between the seeds continues throughout the Old Testament. Though Israel is the covenant people of God, called to be the true and united humanity, conflicts between the seed of the woman and seed of the serpent erupt within Israel. Esau, another Cain, wants to kill Jacob; Joseph's brothers hate him and sell him into slavery; there are battles within Israel after the exodus, and that history of internal conflict hardens into a firm political breach during the period of the kings. Israel, called to reunite the nations, cannot even remain united herself.

When Jesus comes, the Jews are still internally divided, and Jesus, the Seed of the woman, accuses the Jewish leaders of being children of the devil (John 8). The gospel brings in a new human race, where there is neither Jew nor Greek, slave nor free, male nor female. Even now there is still a division in the human race. The New Testament says that there is a radical difference between those who are "inside" and those Gentiles who are "outside." There are two families in the human race, and these two families will remain divided and in conflict until the last day.

This conflict was going on in John's day, and the division took a particular form. On the one side were the deceivers and liars that John labeled antichrists, those who had once been in the church with the apostles and who were now spreading false teaching. On the other side were the children of God. His whole letter is an exhortation to his readers to remain in the one family and not to be seduced or deceived into joining the other family. Echoing in the background is Jesus' sharp confrontation with the Jews in John 8, where he accused them of following the ways of their father, the devil, by lying and murdering (8:31–47). 1 John 3 is the John 8 of his first epistle.

The difference between the seed of the woman and the seed of the serpent is a distinction that God himself makes. The children of God are such because of God's work in them, because God is their Father. For John, this key difference between the children of God and children of the devil manifests itself in a difference of life. This is obvious from the structure of 2:28–3:10, at the center of which is an exhortation to practice righteousness:

A. Little children: abide in him: confidence, righteousness,
    born of God, 2:28–29
  B. Love of Father, children of God, 3:1
    C. We will become like him because we will see him/purity, 3:2–3
      D. Sin and lawlessness, 3:4
        E. Appeared to take away sin, 3:5
          F. No one abiding sins, 3:6
            G. Little children: righteousness, 3:7
          F' Practice sin: of the devil, 3:8a
        E' Son appeared to destroy works of devil, 3:8b
      D' Seed abides; no sin because born of God, 3:9a
    C' Cannot sin because born of God, 3:9b
  B' Children of God/devil, 3:10a
A' Righteousness and love, 3:10b

The section is framed by references to righteousness (*dikaiosunē*), and a cluster of the same word group is found in the center of the passage (v. 7, the *dik-* root used three times). Outside this section *dikaiosunē* is not used at all in 1 John, and the corresponding adjective, *dikaion*, is used prior to this section only in 1:9 and 2:1, with reference to God the Father and to Jesus. This section hangs together by seven clauses that begin "everyone who" (*pas ho*, 2:29, 3:3, 4, 6 [two times], 9, 10),[1] a pattern of seven that indicates that those who are "born of God" are new creations, delivered from the house of their former father, the devil, and adopted by the Father of Jesus the Son.

At the same time, 2:28–3:10 is embedded in a larger structure that covers the entirety of chapter 3. One indication that the themes of this section spill out to 3:11–24 is the fact that the only other use of *dikaion* in the letter occurs in 3:12. Further, love for the brethren, in-

---

1. John Christopher Thomas, "The Literary Structure of 1 John," *Novum Testamentum* 40:4 (1998), 369–81.

troduced first in 3:10, spills over into verses 14–17. Finally, the section is framed by references to the coming (*parousia*) of the Lord and the confidence (*parrēsia*, 2:28, 3:21) that believers have in his presence, as well as by references to "abiding" (*menō*) in him (2:28, 3:24).

This larger section is divided by a series of direct addresses to the readers which alternate between "little children" and some other form of address:

> A. Little children, 2:28
> B. Beloved, 3:2
> A' Little children, 3:7
> C. Brethren, 3:13
> A" Little children, 3:18
> B' Beloved, 3:21

The contents of these various sections fit into this sequence, arranged chiastically.

> A. Righteousness of God's children at his coming, 2:28–3:1
> B. Children of God do not sin, 3:2–6
> C. Children of God/of the devil distinguished by actions to brothers, 3:7–12
> C' World hates brothers; love of brothers, 3:13–17
> B' Love in deed and truth, 3:18–20
> A' Confidence in keeping God's commandments, 3:21–24

The sections can also be arranged in what John Breck describes as a rhetorical helix, as we read in a spiral around the chiasm:

> A. Abide in him in righteousness to have confidence → A' What's more, righteousness is keeping God's commandment to love and believe.
> B. Children of God do not sin → B' What's more, they actively love in deed and truth.
> C. Children of God are not like devilish Cain but practice righteousness in loving brothers → C' What's more, the world hates the brothers, as Cain hated Abel.

110

By the time we get to the end of chapter 3, John has begun to introduce central themes of the following chapter, particularly the Spirit (v. 24). The end of chapter 3 thus functions, like the closing verses of chapter 2, as a hinge, closing out a section and introducing a new one. Chapter 3 not only echoes John 8, but also John 12, Jesus' announcement that he will cast out Satan when he is lifted up on the cross (12:30–32). By the end of chapter 3, though, John is turning toward his epistolary version of the Upper Room Discourse.

BORN OF GOD

1 John 2:28And now, little children, abide in him, so that when he appears we may have confidence and not shrink from him in shame at his coming. 29If you know that he is righteous, you may be sure that everyone who practices righteousness has been born of him.

3:1See what kind of love the Father has given to us, that we should be called children of God; and so we are. The reason why the world does not know us is that it did not know him. 2Beloved, we are God's children now, and what we will be has not yet appeared; but we know that when he appears we shall be like him, because we shall see him as he is. 3And everyone who thus hopes in him purifies himself as he is pure.

4Everyone who makes a practice of sinning also practices lawlessness; sin is lawlessness. 5You know that he appeared to take away sins, and in him there is no sin. 6No one who abides in him keeps on sinning; no one who keeps on sinning has either seen him or known him. 7Little children, let no one deceive you. Whoever practices righteousness is righteous, as he is righteous. 8Whoever makes a practice of sinning is of the devil, for the devil has been sinning from the beginning. The reason the Son of God appeared was to destroy the works of the devil. 9No one born of God makes a practice of sinning, for God's seed abides in him, and he cannot keep on sinning because he has been born of God. 10By this it is evident who are the children of God, and who are the children of the devil: whoever does not practice righteousness is not of God, nor is the one who does not love his brother.

11For this is the message that you have heard from the beginning, that we should love one another. 12We should not be like

Cain, who was of the evil one and murdered his brother. And why did he murder him? Because his own deeds were evil and his brother's righteous. [13]Do not be surprised, brothers, that the world hates you. [14]We know that we have passed out of death into life, because we love the brothers. Whoever does not love abides in death. [15]Everyone who hates his brother is a murderer, and you know that no murderer has eternal life abiding in him. [16]By this we know love, that he laid down his life for us, and we ought to lay down our lives for the brothers. [17]But if anyone has the world's goods and sees his brother in need, yet closes his heart against him, how does God's love abide in him? [18]Little children, let us not love in word or talk but in deed and in truth. [19]By this we shall know that we are of the truth and reassure our heart before him; [20]for whenever our heart condemns us, God is greater than our heart, and he knows everything. [21]Beloved, if our heart does not condemn us, we have confidence before God; [22]and whatever we ask we receive from him, because we keep his commandments and do what pleases him. [23]And this is his commandment, that we believe in the name of his Son Jesus Christ and love one another, just as he has commanded us. [24]Whoever keeps his commandments abides in God, and God in him. And by this we know that he abides in us, by the Spirit whom he has given us.

In 2:29, John describes believers as those who are "born of God" (*ex autou gegennētai*), the first time he uses this phrase in this letter. From here to the end of the letter, however, the notion of birth from God becomes a prominent theme. He uses the phrase twice in 3:9 and connects this birth to love (4:7), belief in Jesus (5:1, two times), victory over the world (5:4), and being guarded from sin (5:4, two times). In 3:9, he also says that the "seed of God" remains in those who have been born of God. God has an eternal Son, eternally begotten of the Father through the Spirit, but now in addition to that eternal Son, God has begotten other sons, other children, also through the Spirit. All the blessings of the Christian life arise, John says, from being "born from God."

What does John mean by this phrase? He clearly is not erasing the difference between Jesus and his disciples. He assumes in his epistles as in his gospel that Jesus is uniquely the Only-Begotten (*monogenē*). In the familial context of 1 John 3 (children, father, brother), John emphasizes that those who are born of God have a family resemblance to their Father. Created in the image of God, those in Christ are born anew, not just to bear the image that Adam defaced but to bear the image of the Last Adam, the better man. Created in the image of light, we are born again to shine with more intense light. The use of the verb "begotten" (*gennaō*) gives us a further clue. In Psalm 2:7, Yahweh declares that he has "this day" begotten his Son who will sit on the throne, and in his first recorded sermon Paul applies this verse to the resurrection of Jesus (Acts 13:33). The Son is eternally begotten, but he was begotten as the glorified God-Man, the Last Adam, the Davidic king, by his resurrection from the dead (cf. Rom. 1:1–4). So too, the children who are born of God in Christ are born again by sharing in his resurrection life by the Spirit. To be born of God is to live as children of light *now*, filled with the light that is God's Light, the Light that is the light of the future endless day. Practically, as John makes clear, this means doing the kinds of things God does—doing righteousness, practicing love, adhering to truth.

Like many of the things John talks about, this privilege of being "born of God" is a distinctively New Covenant gift. Israel was God's son (Ex. 4:23), and the Davidic king was the personalized filial Israel (2 Sam. 7:14). John is saying that those born of God constitute the true Israel, God's fulfilled children. Yet, the new Israel is not simply an expanded old Israel. Israel is never described as being "born of God," and the Davidic king is so described only in Psalm 2. Because the Father has shown himself in the Son, however, and because that Son has been born from the womb of death, those who abide in Christ are his children in a fuller way than Israel was. Every member of the church is in the position of the king of Psalm 2, "begotten" this day, the day of Jesus' resurrection.

At the beginning of chapter 3, John enthusiastically proclaims that this second birth is a manifestation of God's love. The phrase "how great" (*potapēn*) can be translated as "from what country." God's love is surprising, alien, foreign. We normally love things that are lovable and familiar, but God's love is alien because while we were sinners, rebels, and unlovely, God gave his Son for us. So, the difference between the seed of the woman and the seed of the serpent, between the children of God and the children of the devil, is a difference that God makes within the human race.

John also analyzes some of the reasons why the division of the human race, a division that God deepens by begetting us anew through the Spirit, leads to battle and conflict. He analyzes some of the dynamics of the conflict. Verse 3:1 says that we have been born of God, and that is the reason the world does not know us.

"World" here, as we have seen elsewhere in John's letters, refers not to creation or humanity as such, but humanity and human culture organized in rebellion against God. Specifically, "world" refers to the Jews, since in their rebellion they are at the center of the "world." In this passage, the world includes all those who have not been born of God, or those who are children of the devil. Because the world doesn't know the Father, because the world doesn't know the God who gave us birth, the world doesn't know us either. We are strange and alien to the world, as strange and alien as the love of God that begot us.

In the early centuries of the church, many pagans complained about the bizarre customs of the Christians. Christians were accused of atheism because they didn't worship the traditional gods. They were accused of incest because they greeted one another with a holy kiss, and because of their familial familiarity with one another and their use of kin language to describe the church. They were accused of cannibalism because they met together to eat and drink Jesus' body and blood. It shouldn't be surprising when the world attributes all kinds of evil things to us. They attribute all sorts of base motives. This is to be expected. They don't know our Father, and since we are begotten of God, we bear some resemblance to the Father. They are going to misunderstand us as well.

Unfortunately, the modern church has too often tried hard to avoid being strange. Modern Christians have adjusted to the world's standards. We don't want to sound unscientific, so we find ways to reinterpret Genesis 1 so it fits with current scientific theory. We don't want to look odd, so we conform our fashion sense to that of the world, without considering whether or not God has something to say about our clothing. We don't want to be uncool, so our tastes become identical to the world. This makes things a lot easier. There's no conflict between the church and the world when the church imitates the world. We don't seem alien and strange, as if we have come from another planet, but we are acting against our nature: we are children of God, children of the resurrection, but we behave the same as the children of the devil, as if we were still in the same old dead flesh as everyone else.

Verse 13 goes further: not only does the world regard us as enigmatic, but it hates us. This should not surprise us, and John points to the example of Cain in verse 12 to show that the world's hostility against the righteous is nearly as ancient as man. Children have hated other children as long as there have been children.

Verse 12 points to another aspect of this situation: the world hates the righteous precisely for being righteous. Cain didn't hate Abel for his wickedness; Cain hated Abel because Abel was righteous, and Cain was wicked. Besides, Abel spoke to Cain, and Cain hated him for his rebuke (Gen. 4:8). Cain hated Abel because Abel was acceptable to God and Cain wasn't. No doubt Cain characterized Abel's righteousness as self-righteousness and pride, but John tells us that it was Abel's genuine righteousness that provoked the murderous rage of his brother.

John displays a subtle understanding of psychology here. When we are in the presence of a genuinely righteous person, we feel condemned. They don't have to say or do anything to condemn us; we just feel condemned. To justify ourselves, to relieve ourselves of the condemnation we feel, we attack them and hate them. If we can make them seem less righteous by slandering them or finding some chink in their armor, we can let ourselves off the hook. Worse, we might try to eliminate them, either literally killing them or figuratively murdering them by excluding them from our lives.

Ultimately, this phenomenon is rooted in the central thread of John's letter. God is Light, and as Light he has shone into the dark places of the world, exposing them so they can be judged. We are children of God, and therefore children of Light, and what God is, so we are in the world (cf. 4:17). As we practice righteousness, God's light shines through us and exposes the sins of the world around us. Just as men cower in darkness when the eternal Light steps onto the stage, so men cower and cover and attack when he shines in and through his church. Begotten of God like Abel, we expose and shame the Cains of this world.

LAWLESSNESS AND RIGHTEOUSNESS

John emphasizes that the difference between the two families is not just a difference of origin, but a difference in practice. If we are children of the devil, then we will follow his works, and be liars and murderers. If we are children of God, we will practice righteousness. What we are is evident in what we do. It is not only that we do what we are—that we act in accord with our nature. The reverse is also the case: we are what we do.

John describes the conduct of the children of the devil as "practicing sin" (*ho poiōn tēn hamartian*) and says that "sin is lawlessness" (*anomia*). This is sometimes translated so that it appears John defines sin as transgression of the written law. That's not what the Greek text says. The Greek text doesn't use the word "law" or the verb "transgress." John actually writes, "everyone who practices sin practices lawlessness; and sin is lawlessness."

Lawlessness is not just breaking specific commandments. Rather, lawlessness leads to breaking commandments. Lawlessness is rebellion, the rejection of authority and commandments as such. Someone can be a perfectly law-abiding citizen in one sense, observing all the written rules, and still be a lawless rebel. John is not defining sin merely in terms of violation of a written code. God has graciously committed his will to writing in Scripture. He has showed us in detail, and in a permanent written form, what it means to be righteous. However, the essence of righteousness is faithfulness to *God*, and the essence of sin is personal rebellion against him. This means too that sin is not merely a failure or a lapse (in Hebrew, a *hattat*). Sin is an active rebellion against God.

That's the kind of behavior that characterizes the children of the devil. Satan was lawless from the beginning, a rebel, a boundary-breaker who assaulted the limits given him. Children of Satan continue that lawlessness and rebellion, that rejection of God and his authority. As we have already noted, the children of God are characterized by their behavior too. John insists that righteousness must be manifest in conduct. Those who have hope in God purify themselves, and the ones who abide in him do not sin (vv. 3, 9). He warns against the antichrists who would deceive his readers into thinking they could be righteous without practicing righteousness. They can't. The one who is born of God does not practice sin, and cannot sin, precisely because he is born of God. There is no such thing as a rebel who has been born of God. Someone who claims to be born of God and rebels against him is not born of God to begin with. He is a liar, and therefore a child of the chief liar, Satan.

John may well be challenging Jews and Judaizers here. For many Jews, righteousness was a status that came with being Jewish. To be circumcised and brought into the covenant with Israel gave one a permanent status of being righteous. Yet, Jesus accused the Jews of being wicked, robbing widows and substituting their own laws for the commandments of God. They claimed to have a righteous status as Jews, but they did not practice righteousness. Paul too challenges Jews who claim a status by virtue of circumcision but nullify circumcision by their disobedience (Rom. 2). John makes the same point.

Righteousness can be a legal term that describes the status of someone that the judge has judged to be in the right. In John's usage, however, the point is not about *status* but *life*. As John says in verse 7, "the one who practices righteousness is righteous, just as He is righteous." Being righteous means practicing righteousness. In that sense righteousness has to do with faithfulness to the terms of a covenant relationship. A husband is righteous when he conforms to the demands of his marital covenant with his wife, and one born of God is righteous when he conforms to the demands of the covenant relationship with God. Righteousness does mean avoiding sin—not breaking the commandments of God—but righteousness also involves active pursuit of justice and generosity. Righteousness shows itself in sharing goods with those who have none (v. 17). Righteousness is not "strict justice" as opposed to mercy. Practicing righteousness or justice means relieving the oppressed and breaking the yoke of the oppressor—both acts of mercy.

John is not saying that Christians are sinless. He goes so far as to say that those who are born of God "cannot sin" (3:9), but earlier he said that anyone who claims to be sinless is a liar and makes God a liar (1:8, 10). John hasn't contradicted himself. In 3:9, he's talking about the general tone of our way of living. Those who are born of God are characterized by righteous conduct, while those who are children of the devil are dominated by sin.

WORKS OF THE DEVIL

How can we live up to the demands that John is placing on us? How can we ever be righteous as God is righteous, pure as he is pure? John answers by pointing to the source of power for practicing righteousness and overcoming sin. Not only are we born of God, but we can be righteous in action because of the appearances of Jesus. Twice John refers to the past appearance of Jesus, the coming of the Son of God in his incarnation, life, death and resurrection. Jesus appeared, John says here, for two reasons. Jesus appeared to destroy things, to remove things, to judge the world. He came to take away sin (v. 5). This doesn't refer to Jesus dying as our substitute to remove the guilt of sin. John's concern here is with practice, and the sin that Jesus takes away is the sin that dominates our lives and makes us do things we don't want to do. Jesus, the Sinless One, comes to destroy sin, to remove it, to rob it of its power. Because the sinless Jesus has taken away sin, we are able to practice righteousness and not rebellion.

Jesus also came to "destroy the works of the devil" (v 8). John's language here is exodus language. Jesus came to "loose" us from the devil, to liberate us from the devil's mastery, who held us in bondage worse than Pharaoh's. Jesus is the greater Moses, who

118

destroys the works of the devil so that we don't share in the rebelliousness of the father of murder and lies. Jesus delivers children of the devil to make them children of God, just as Yahweh came to Israel to deliver his "son" from Egypt. We are able to practice righteousness because of what Jesus accomplished in his first appearance. We cannot escape the devil's power on our own. Jesus has done that for us.

John also refers to a future appearance of Jesus in verse 2, and in verse 3 indicates that this future appearance is one of the motivations for our purification and righteousness. Because we hope for the appearance of Jesus, we seek *now* to be pure, as he himself is without any stain of sin. Traditionally, this passage is taken as a reference to Jesus' final coming. Jesus will eventually appear, at the end of all things, and when we see him in this appearance we will be transformed into his likeness. This is certainly possible. And it's true that Jesus is coming at the end of all things, to defeat the last enemy, death, and to raise up the dead to share in his resurrection life. Given the overall context of the letter, however, it is more likely that John is still referring to an imminent appearance, Jesus coming within an "hour" of time to inspect and judge. When he comes then, the church will be transformed and what we shall be shall appear. John's readers are already children, but when Jesus appears, he will share his inheritance. With his coming at the end of the old age, the church is transfigured into a new form, and she begins to share more fully in the life that is in him. With his appearance, he completes his progress from darkness into light, his emergence from hiding.

Whatever John is referring to specifically, the ethical import is the same. Knowing that we have a hope in Jesus that we will be like him, we purify ourselves. When we are born of God, we are born to hope. We look forward to God's appearance, and to the transfiguration we'll experience when he appears, a transfiguration that surpasses all we can imagine (3:2). Our lives as Christians are lived out between Christ's appearances. He appeared once to destroy sin and the devil's works; and we live in faith that he has done that. He comes regularly to inspect and judge; and we live in hope for his coming. He will come again at the end of all things to set everything right and to raise us from the dead; and as this is our hope, we purify ourselves as he is pure.

CAINITES

Early on in 1 John, we learn that the churches John addresses are troubled. We have an inkling that the world is a seductive lure for some in the church. As the book progresses, the world changes from seductive to threatening, and as the letter winds its circuitous way toward the center, we get a better idea of the causes of trouble. John's churches are enduring persecution, and persecution causes division. In chapter 3, he uses the figure of Cain from Genesis 4 to describe the "world" that hates believers (vv. 12–13).

Cain is the first persecutor in the Bible, the first murderer, but there are other reasons why John would choose to compare the persecutors of the church with Cain. For starters, we should not take the reference to murder metaphorically, as if John were talking about hatred and anger but using the metaphor of murder to describe it. He does say that everyone who hates his brother is a murderer, but when he mentions Cain he's talking about actual killing.[2] Cain slew his brother, and the Cainites that John is talking about are literally killing believers. Cain fits the situation because the Christians John writes to are in mortal danger from their persecutors. A reference to Cain is also fitting because of Cain's relationship to Abel. Cain was an older brother who attacked his righteous younger brother.

In this Cain was also the first of a series. Older brothers frequently attack younger brothers in the Old Testament. Ishmael mocks Isaac. Esau hates and wants to kill Jacob, so Jacob has to flee. Joseph is one of the younger sons of Jacob, and his brothers hate and plan to kill him before finally sending him off in slavery to

---

2. Much of this was inspired by Jeff Meyers's superb lectures on the epistle of James at a recent Biblical Horizons Summer Conference.

Egypt. David's brothers charge him with being insolent and wicked, and Solomon's brother Adonijah seeks to wrest the throne from him. There are a few counter-examples in the Old Testament, the chief of which is Jonathan: he is the heir-apparent to the throne of Saul, brother-in-law to David — older by perhaps a generation — and yet he willingly cedes his position as crown prince to honor David. Ultimately, Jesus comes as the younger Adam, the new David, and his older brothers, the Jews, slay him.

Whenever the older-brother theme appears in the New Testament, it's normally connected to the division between outcast Jews and insider Jews, or between Jews and Gentiles. When Jesus tells the parable of the prodigal son, the older brother stands for the Pharisees who refuse to rejoice that prodigal "sinners" are returning to their father's house (Luke 15), and Jesus tells a variation of this story when he tells the parable of the workmen in the vineyard (Matt. 20:1–16). Some arrive to work early in the morning, some at the third hour, some at the sixth, some at the ninth, and the last ones at the eleventh hour. When the owner of the vineyard pays them, he pays them all the same amount, but the ones who have worked since early morning complain that they deserve more. They are like the grumbling, persecuting older brother in the prodigal son parable. In both parables, Jesus is depicting the murmuring of pure Jews who don't like Jesus hanging around with people who have been eating from pig troughs. Similarly, when Paul allegorizes on the story of Isaac and Ishmael, these two sons of Abraham become emblematic of two covenants, one of flesh and one of promise (Gal. 4:21–31), and when Paul talks about Jacob and Esau in Romans 9, and says that the Lord promised that the elder would serve the younger, he is again talking about the relationship of fleshly Israel—the Old Covenant people of God—with the church of the New Covenant.

These Old Testament types fit exactly the situation of persecution in the first-century church. The Jews had been the Lord's people for two millennia, and now along come these Johnny-come-lately Gentiles and they claim to have received the Abrahamic promise. How dare they claim to be righteous Abel? We are the firstborn, the Jews protest, forgetting that Cain was the firstborn. Cain, who assaulted his adult brother's community as well as his brother, is the perfect figure of the persecuting older brother, the prototype of all later persecutors, everyone who sheds blood from Abel to Zechariah the son of Berechiah.

John uses a verb in verse 12 that might be translated as "butcher" (*esfaxen*) and which has sacrificial connotations. Cain didn't just murder his brother; he offered the first human sacrifice and slaughtered Abel as a religious act. Cain saw that his own works were evil, and his brother's were righteous, and he killed Abel in a vain effort to atone for his sin. That too fits with the situation of the first-century Christians. As Jesus said, predicting the events of what he called the last days, "They will make you outcasts from the synagogue, but an hour is coming for everyone who kills you to think he is offering service to God" (John 16:2). The Jews thought the survival of Israel depended on destroying the church. Like Phinehas, they were purging the holy camp of Israel by slaughtering the fornicating followers of this false Messiah, Jesus. This was certainly Paul's form of zealotry, until Jesus arrested his persecution by confronting him on the Damascus Road.

Sacrifice is inescapable in human life. We think we've outgrown sacrifice, but human sacrifice still happens every day. Husbands offended by their wives' correction take vengeance at the first opportunity; siblings cut each other down with words sharp as swords; envious employees slander one of their fellows to keep him from advancing. When three siblings gang up against one and feel the pleasure of uniting in torturing him, they are butchers, and when a church blames all its problems on one troublesome member or a group of members or the pastor, they have turned those members or the pastor into scapegoats. Beyond these low-level forms of human sacrifice, terrorists keep their cause going by blood and carnage, and nations wreak their vengeance on their neighbors with smart bombs and surface-to-air rockets.

The alternative is not to avoid sacrifice altogether. That is impossible. The solution, rather, is to act like Jesus rather than Cain. My colleague John Schwandt points out that John puns on "Cain"

(*Kain*) and the pronoun that refers to Jesus (*ekeinos*, v. 16), which means "that one" and sounds like "ekainos." Instead of butchering others like Cain, "that one," Jesus, gave his own life on behalf of others. We are to imitate Jesus' self-sacrifice. Instead of sacrificing others to make things even, we sacrifice ourselves, taking the second strike on the left cheek.

We are not only to imitate, but are to rest in Christ's work. Guilt demands satisfaction. When we are gripped with guilt, we look for someone to slaughter, but we have no need for any victim. Jesus has died once for all, and we can imitate him only if we trust in his once-for-all death. His blood cleanses us from all sin. All of our butchering of one another, all of our scapegoating, all of our sacrificing of others arises from unbelief, from our failure to trust the one scapegoat, the sacrifice of the cross that ends all sacrifice. Only through the sacrifice of Jesus can humans end both the tiny and titanic sacrifices that occur daily in human society.

This sort of murderous hatred is not uncommon, John says, and we should not be surprised when the world hates us. Cainites have hated Abelites from the beginning and will until the end of the world. The question is not whether the world will hate and persecute, but how we will respond to it. This is particularly where John's instructions take on a universal force. It seemed perfectly natural to someone in the first century to react violently to persecution. Jews reacted quickly and violently to any kind of attack, and so did their pagan neighbors. They were extremely sensitive to insult, and extremely quick to slash back. Honor was one of their chief values, and any damage to honor had to be redressed, immediately and severely. With the rest of the New Testament, John rejects the honor ethic of ancient man, making it clear that the response to the hatred of the world cannot be hatred in return. In fact, if we respond to the hatred of the world with hatred, then we have actually joined the Cainites, those who persecute and murder.

John's main concern, though, is not with how Christians behave toward the worldly Cainites who slaughter the church and think they do service to God. He is more concerned about the way Christians, under the threat of persecution and slaughter, treat each other. He knows that the members of the church, pressured by persecution, will be tempted to turn on each other, and begin blaming, scapegoating, and slaughtering one another. That is strategically disastrous, of course, because it weakens the church, but that is not John's main fear. He says that if we turn on one another when the world pressures us, we have become just another outpost of the world. If we hate our brothers, we become murderers just as surely as Cain was a murderer.

For John, love is not an optional ornament to human life. It is literally an issue of life and death. Without love—specifically without the self-sacrificial love of Jesus—human beings cannot live together well, if at all. That is why the mark that we have passed from the death of the "world" into the "life" of the body of Christ is the love that we show for one another. Because we think of "life" as primarily biological, we tend to think that we are still alive even if our lives are full of hatred, envy, and anger. John defines life as fellowship with God (John 17:3), and says that if we are not walking in love we are dead. And not just dead. If we hate our brothers, we are murderers (vv. 14–15), performing a kind of macabre evangelism that gathers the dead into a community of death. When we hate brothers, we become mirror images of the persecutors. The only alternative, John says, is imitating Christ in giving ourselves to the brothers (v. 16). That is still a death. There is going to be "death" regardless: the choice is whether we "kill" our brothers through our hate or give our own lives to and for them (v. 16). Either we make our brothers scapegoats and murder them, or we offer ourselves in sacrifice for them.

What does it mean, in concrete terms, to imitate Christ in giving up our lives for the brothers? John, using Christ as the model for Christian virtue in verse 17, tells us Jesus had all the "world's goods" as his own, but gave them up for us. He who was rich, for our sake he became poor. If we are truly in him, and he in us, this will manifest itself in open-hearted generosity. We have received the Spirit who is the Gift of God, and when the Spirit dwells in us, he gives himself through us, and makes giving the keynote of our lives. John specifically has material wealth in mind, and he urges his readers to imitate not only Jesus but the early church, where Christians sold houses and other property to help their poor brothers. But wealth comes in many forms (talents, for instance), and John says that we should use this wealth to help a brother in need. This is the form that love must take if it is to be genuine love. James makes the same point: "What does it profit, my brethren, if someone says he has faith but does not have works? Can faith save him? If a brother or sister is naked and destitute of daily food, and one of you says to them, 'Depart in peace, be warmed and filled,' but you do not give them the things which are needed for the body, what does it profit? Thus also faith by itself, if it does not have works, is dead" (Jas. 2:14ff.).

The earliest Christians took this demand so literally that they sold their personal property, voluntarily giving up houses, land, and other wealth so they could help their brothers and sisters in need. It is no faith at all if it does not act with generosity and charity.

Think again of the concrete situation John deals with. Worldly Cains—vicious persecutors—are attacking the church. When the persecutors come and drag a man off, they leave widows and orphans behind. The church is full of families and wives and children who have been victimized by the persecution. John says that love for the brothers must not be merely in word but in deed. It's not enough to express sympathy for a brother who is having a financial crisis; love means giving him assistance. This is the way of life, the life of those begotten, like Jesus, from God the Father—being willing to give up the "world's life" (*bios*, v. 17) for one another.

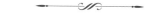

KNOWING THAT WE KNOW

John ends this section by returning to the theme of assurance. As in chapter 2, he speaks of knowledge, using the phrase "we know that" several times: we know that we have passed from death to life because we love the brethren (v 14); "we know we are of the truth" if we open our lives and hands in generous service to the brothers (v 19); we know that he abides in us through the Spirit if we keep his commandments (v 24). Assurance was no doubt a particular problem in John's day. Jews claimed to be the true people of God and believed that they were the chosen, and they had a historical pedigree to prove it. They attacked the Christians who claimed to be the true Israel. The weight of tradition was definitely on the side of the Jews, the elder brothers. Christians were upstarts. Especially when the heat started turning up, Christians would be tempted to doubt whether Jesus really was who he said he was, whether following Jesus was really worth the trouble. Maybe the Jews were right. Maybe we should join them.

John wants to reassure his readers that they are on the right side of this conflict, something that can become questionable under the pressure of persecution. How does he assure them? John certainly doesn't want us to find assurance by withdrawing into our hearts and looking for repose there. That is the *opposite* of what he encourages. We come to know by walking in love, and walking in love leads us *out of ourselves* to assurance. John knows that our hearts often condemn us (3:20), often for small errors that are not worthy of condemnation. However, the condemnation of our hearts is not the final issue with assurance. "God is greater than our hearts" (v. 20). Whether our hearts condemn us or not, God gives us assurance that we are in the truth *as* we walk in love. Through loving our brothers we come to experience the assurance that "we are of the truth" (v. 19). As in 2:3, "know" in 3:19 has the sense of "experience." We come to know in our bones that we belong to Jesus when we love the brothers and keep his commandments. As we imitate Christ in giving ourselves and our goods for the brothers, we experience that we are in the truth, the realm of life.

When our hearts are assured by God, we have confidence in prayer. We can ask whatever we want because we keep his commandments and live in a way pleasing to God (3:22). John is not talking about "works righteousness," as if we could coerce God into doing us favors by our good works. But he *does* say there is a causal connection between effective prayer and obedience: "whatever we ask we receive from Him, because [*hoti*] we keep His commandments." If your prayers are not being answered, examine yourself. Ask if you are walking in obedience. If you want God to open his ear to you, open your ears to him.

John emphasizes throughout his letter that Christians must obey God's commandments. In this, he only repeats what Jesus said. Jesus said, if you love me, keep my commandments. That's all that John is saying. He's not saying that we earn our standing with God. He is simply saying that obedience is the Christian way of life.

The way of obedience is also a way of intimate fellowship with God. In verse 24, John writes that the one who keeps God's commandments abides in God, and God abides in him. John does not think of God up in heaven monitoring our obedience down on earth. John is not saying that God observes our behavior from a distance and is either pleased with it or not. John does not believe God is imprisoned in some Deistic fourth dimension. John says the way of obedience is not only the way to please God, not only the way of Christian living. It is also the way of mutual abiding in God through the Spirit. As we obey his commandments, we remain in him, and he remains in us. When we walk in obedience, we become a dwelling place for God, and he becomes our dwelling place. As we obey his commandments, we are united with God in the way that God is united with himself: just as the Father is eternally in the Son through the Spirit, and the Son eternally in the Father through the Spirit, so as we obey the commandments of God we abide in him and he in us. Obeying God's commandments is the way of intimate mutual indwelling. When we obey, God is our home, and we are his; as we obey, God makes room for us in himself, and makes room for himself in us.

8

TEST THE SPIRITS
1 John 4:1–6

¹ John 4:1Beloved, do not believe every spirit, but test the spirits to see whether they are from God, for many false prophets have gone out into the world. ²By this you know the Spirit of God: every spirit that confesses that Jesus Christ has come in the flesh is from God, ³and every spirit that does not confess Jesus is not from God. This is the spirit of the antichrist, which you heard was coming and now is in the world already. ⁴Little children, you are from God and have overcome them, for he who is in you is greater than he who is in the world. ⁵They are from the world; therefore they speak from the world, and the world listens to them. ⁶We are from God. Whoever knows God listens to us; whoever is not from God does not listen to us. By this we know the Spirit of truth and the spirit of error.

The first six verses of 1 John 4 are arranged chiastically:

A. Test spirits, verse 1
  B. Confession, verses 2–3
    C. From God/the world, verses 3b–4a
      D. We overcome them, verse 4b
    C' From God/from world, verses 5–6a
  B' Hearing (*akouō*), verse 6b
A' Spirits, verse 6c

John's direct address to the readers as little children (v. 4) reinforces the conclusion that this is the central section of the passage. John assures the little children that they will overcome because they originate from God. They are all little children because they are all begotten of God. The contrast of B and B' is also intriguing. The false prophets who deny that Jesus has come from God are further described as being from the world (v. 5) and having an audience in the world (v. 5). They refuse to listen to the apostles (v. 6b). False prophets and lying spirits are known not only by what they confess, but by their audience and by their influences. We must certainly ask what teachers are saying and teaching, but John also teaches us to ask who is listening to *them*. And to whom are *they* listening? Whose *shema* do they profess?

Though the text does fall out as a chiasm, its structure is far more complex. It moves in a cascading spiral that winds around the chiasm, like Celtic marginal illuminations, twinings on twinings. Though John focuses attention on listening in verse 6, the word "hear" is already used in verse 5, wrapping around the contrast of from the world (5a) and from God (6a). Verses 5–6 could thus be outlined as:

A. They are from the world
  B. The world hears them
A' We are from God
  B' Whoever knows God hears us

There are two melody lines going simultaneously, a chiastic return to the beginning and a cyclical line that twists and turns around the chiasm like ivy. The phrase "from God" is also used six times in verses 1–6, and a seventh in verse 7, the only uses of the phrase in 1 John. This is another example of the twisting cyclical rhetoric of John's letter. Verse 7 begins a new section, since it begins with a direct address ("beloved") and turns to the theme of love. Yet John uses the phrase "from God" in verse 7, binding together his exhortation to love (love being "from God") with the references to spirits that are/are not "from God." Love becomes yet another test of whether a spirit is from God.

The word "spirit" (*pneuma*) is used seven times in verses 1–6 (and hinted at once, in verse 3: literally, "the of-the-antichrist"). This is the great passage about the Spirit in 1 John, rivaling the Upper Room Discourse in John's gospel. Interestingly, only one of the uses (v. 2) is unambiguously a reference to the Holy Spirit. John describes a battle of spirits, and is confident that the Spirit of God will be victorious. Further, the first use of the word "spirit" in the book comes in 3:24, and between that use and the end of the letter John uses "spirit" twelve times, a hint that this is the Spirit of the new Israel. Verses 1–6 also use the word "world" six times, but the six-fold world will be overcome by the seven-fold Spirit.

DISCERNMENT AND LOVE

Commentators sometimes suggest that 1 John 4:1–6 marks a rupture in John's argument. Verse 3:23 speaks of love as a commandment of God. There is no mention of love in 4:1–6, but then John resumes the discussion of love in verse 7. Some have gone so far as to say that 4:1–6 is a later interpolation. Taking the text as it stands, however, the exhortation to test the spirits is embedded within the commandment to love one another. The connections of love and discernment are manifold. John teaches that discernment is possible because of "He who is in you" (4:4), the "spirit of truth" (4:6). This Spirit is the one through whom God abides in us and we in him, and by whom love abides in us (4:12–13). In short, discernment and love both have the same source—the abiding Spirit.

Everyone knows judgmental, "discerning" theological bullies who want to display their superiority and cut others down. Properly exercised, however, judgment/testing is an act of love, intended to prevent others from falling into deadly errors. Just as there is no conflict between the gift of teaching and the gift of service in the church, so there is no conflict between the gift of discernment and the gift of love. The Spirit is one, and his gifts are harmonious. Love and judgment are both rooted in the gospel announcement: the God who comes out of hiding in his Word comes in love but also comes as light, the searching light of judicial scrutiny. These are not opposed to each other, but are both effects of God's emergence from the darkness.

There may also be something of an epistemological point here. It is not simply that we *ought* to exercise discernment out of love for one another. It's also the case that we cannot exercise proper discernment well without love. We might think that we see clearly even if we do not love, but John doesn't agree. The late Richard Neuhaus is fond of quoting Martin Luther King, Jr.'s claim that anyone who brings a message of prophetic condemnation must first love those to whom he prophesies. Without love, we cannot test spirits rightly. As we noted in chapter 4, hatred clouds judgment. Hateful people become stupid.

Finally, 4:1–6 highlights one dimension of John's understanding of love. John has been interpreted as an apostle of sentimental affection. He is definitely an apostle of love (so is Paul, of course), but the love that he encourages is not a soft tolerance or squishy acceptance. John inserts an exhortation to agnosticism and unbelief ("do not believe," 4:1)—a command to discern, examine, and judge—into a passage dealing with love. For John, love is not absolute toleration, unconditional welcome, boundary-less hospitality. Discernment should be loving, but at the same time love must be discerning.

FALSE PROPHETS

False prophets appeared in Israel mainly near the time of the fall of Jerusalem and Judah, during the days of Jeremiah (14:13–18; 23:16–22) and Ezekiel (13:1–23). According to Jeremiah, everyone at the time was "greedy for gain"; from prophet to priest, all were willing to deal falsely for money (Jer. 6:13; 8:10). False prophets in Jeremiah's time prophesied that Judah and Jerusalem would be at peace, that the Babylonians would be turned back, and that Yahweh would at the last deliver his people and city. They prophesied "peace, peace," but there was no peace (Jer. 6:14; 8:11). It's not surprising that Jeremiah had to contend with false prophets. False prophets thrive on times of calamity. When the world seems to be falling apart, people flail around for someone who seems to know what is happening. Or, they look for people who reassure them that everything is going to be all right, that it will be "peace, peace" for the foreseeable future. During times of crisis and uncertainty, prophecy is big business. (Who wouldn't want to take a peek if someone wrote a book claiming to predict stock market trends for the next ten years?)

Crisis and false prophecy have recurred in tandem throughout the history of the church. As the first millennium AD wound down, many predicted that the world was going to end. During the fourteenth century, when Europe appeared to be overrun by the horsemen of the Apocalypse, when plague killed one-third of the population of Europe, and war and schism were the order of the day, there was an outbreak of millennial, apocalyptic prophecy. The world was ending, and the prophets of doom seemed to know for sure. They offered hope that the suffering had a reason, and that things would soon turn out better.

John's time was similar. The last hour had come, and antichrists were abroad in the land. There was a sense of crisis and doom, of impending catastrophe. We don't know exactly when John wrote his letter, but it was likely sometime in the late 60s AD, perhaps after the outbreak of the Jewish War that ended with the Roman sack of Jerusalem and the destruction of Herod's temple. As usual, this time of catastrophe brought out the prophets, and the New Testament is full of warnings about the dangers of false prophets and the need to resist them.

"Beware the false prophets," Jesus said, "who are like wolves in sheep's clothing" (Matt. 7:10). Peter warned that false teachers would arise in the church, just as false prophets arose in Israel: "false prophets also arose among the people, just as there will also be false teachers among you, who will secretly introduce destructive heresies, even denying the Master who bought them, bringing swift destruction upon themselves" (2 Pet. 2:1).

Jesus connected the rise of false prophets specifically to the coming of the end, the final destruction of the old order, and the coming of the new order. "Many false prophets will arise and will mislead many" (Matt. 24:11), he said, and "false Christs and false prophets will arise and will show great signs and wonders, so as to mislead, if possible, even the elect" (Matt. 24:24).

BATTLE OF SPIRITS

As John sees things, false prophecy is not merely a sociological phenomenon. It's not merely a power struggle or a response to social upheaval. Invisible spiritual forces are at work. False prophets are not simply human agents, motivated by their own desires and shaped by the cultural environment. These factors certainly affect their actions, but John says that fundamentally they are agents of various sorts of "spirits" (vv. 1–2). As in the court of Ahab (1 Kings 22), the contest of true and false prophecy is not a contest between the spirit and no spirit. It's a contest of the Spirit of truth and lying spirits. As John says at the end of this passage, the church must distinguish between the "Spirit of truth" and "spirits of error." The battle raging in the first century, in other words, was not merely between the apostles and the Judaizers. The battle was between the Spirit and the demonic spirits of the kingdom of darkness. What John describes is a literal Spiritual warfare, one that precedes an assault on Jerusalem like the assault of Nebuchadnezzar.

Of course, these warnings are still relevant to us today. False prophets have continued to arise throughout the history of the church. Even in our sophisticated, scientific age, many are attracted to spiritualities and cults that teach a false gospel and mislead many. Satan is defeated, but he stupidly fights on, hoping to pull out a victory at the last. What is going on in the Episcopal church is not merely a battle between conservatives who want to maintain traditional Christian morality and libertines who want to make room for sodomy in high places. It is a battle of spirits; it is an attempt at a hostile takeover, an effort by satanic forces to transform the Episcopal church into a synagogue of Satan.

This can happen on a smaller scale, too. Paul warns us not to let the sun go down on our anger, because if we do we give the devil an opportunity (Eph. 4). This doesn't mean simply that if we retain anger we become accusers, as Satan is an accuser. It doesn't only mean that anger makes us devilish slanderers (the Greek word for devil, *diabolon*, means slanderer). We do become accusers and slanderers when we are angry, but Paul should be taken literally. Satan is given an opportunity to turn you into an ally if you don't deal with your anger, confess sin, forgive, and extend forgiveness. If you fail here, Satan has an opportunity to infect your marriage, your relations with your co-workers, your relationship with others at church.

Not everyone who claims to speak for God does speak for God. But how can we tell? In part, we can tell by a prophet's accuracy. Success is a standard of judgment. Deuteronomy 18 says that a prophet whose predictions do not come to pass is to be stoned:

> "[T]he prophet who presumes to speak a word in My name, which I have not commanded him to speak, or who speaks in the name of other gods, that prophet shall die." And if you say in your heart, "How shall we know the word which the LORD has not spoken?"—when a prophet speaks in the name of the LORD, if the thing does not happen or come to pass, that is the thing which the LORD has not spoken; the prophet has spoken it presumptuously; you shall not be afraid of him. (Deut. 18:20–22)

What does this mean for men who present themselves as prophecy experts, men like Pat Robertson, who announced a few years ago that the Lord had told him what would happen in the coming year? Or Hal Lindsey, who has been predicting the end is coming for several decades, based on a fanciful misreading of Revelation and other books? Are these men false prophets who should be rejected? By biblical standards, the answer is yes. Whatever good Robertson and Lindsey have done, they have made predictions about the future that are false. I am not claiming that they are unbelievers, but they do labor under delusions that are demonically inspired, and they ought not be teachers in the church. We should not listen to them.

Beyond that, both the Torah and John say that spirits and prophets are to be tested by their tongue and their ears, by what they confess, and by whom they listen to. According to the law, a false prophet was identifiable by the fact that he called for people to follow other gods. Deuteronomy 13 says,

> if there arises among you a prophet or a dreamer of dreams, and he gives you a sign or a wonder, and the sign or the wonder comes to pass, of which he spoke to you, saying, "Let us go after other gods"—which you have not known—"and let us serve them," you shall not listen to the words of that prophet or that dreamer of dreams, for the LORD your God is testing you to know whether you love the LORD your God with all your heart and with all your soul. You shall walk after the LORD your God and fear Him, and keep His commandments and obey His voice; you shall serve Him and hold fast to Him. But that prophet or that dreamer of dreams shall be put to death, because he has spoken in order to turn you away from the LORD your God, who brought you out of the land of Egypt and redeemed you from the house of bondage, to entice you from the way in which the LORD your God commanded you to walk. So you shall put away the evil from your midst.

John likewise gives a theological test. Everyone who confesses with his tongue that Jesus has come in the flesh is of God (v. 2). The Holy Spirit, somewhat strangely, is known by his testimony to the *flesh* of Jesus. Spirits that deny Jesus is God in the flesh, that Jesus is Christ-in-flesh, are anti-Christ (v. 3; cf. 2:18, 22). This could be seen as a New Covenant application of Deuteronomy 13. Denying that Jesus-incarnate is from God, denying that he is Yahweh himself living as man, denying that Jesus is the Word of Life who was from the beginning, is tantamount to denying God, and tantamount to saying, "let us go after other gods." Prophets who urge us to worship another God than the one revealed in Jesus are false prophets. Prophets who urge us to worship God while ignoring Jesus are false prophets. Judaizers who say "let us follow Moses and not Jesus" are false prophets. We could put it in trinitarian terms. The Holy Spirit glorifies the Son and the Father. The spirit of antichrist does the opposite: it denigrates the Son and in doing so denies the Father. Saying Jesus is not God in flesh is Judaizing Gnosticism, because it implies that Yahweh has not shown himself, not made himself available for us.

For John, false prophecy is not merely a matter of the mouth. The tongue speaks what is in the heart, and the heart is also manifested in action. "Antichrist" names not only a doctrinal heresy, but also a lifestyle characterized by unrighteousness and hatred for brothers (3:10–12). Anyone who causes strife among the brothers is antichrist, denying in effect that Jesus has come in the flesh. When we don't honor and love the fleshly brothers who are born of the Spirit of Jesus, we hate the very flesh of the Son of God. We become heretics just as truly as if we turned Arian or Apollinarian.

False prophets are also known by ears (vv. 5–6). This works two ways. On the one hand, false prophets find eager ears in the world. Tongue and ear make a pair. Lying spirits speak from the world, and the ears that listen are also worldly. The world listens to them because they speak from the world (v. 5). So, one test of false teaching is to ask who listens to them. Of course, success isn't necessarily a sign of falsehood. Jesus drew great crowds. But if a prophet receives approval from people who live according to the flesh, who are dominated by the lust of the eyes, the lust of the flesh, and the boastful pride of life—that's a sign that the prophet is a false prophet. On the other hand, false prophets open their ears to something other than the apostolic voice. John makes the astounding claim that "the one who knows God hears us" (v. 6). Listening to the apostles is a test of whether someone is a child of God or a child of the devil. This claim is even more astounding if, as seems likely, John is alluding to the Jewish *shema* ("Hear!"). Israel is knowable as the people that respond to Yahweh's "Hear, O Israel"; the new Israel is known as the people that respond to the apostolic "Hear."

We live in a dazzling carnival of religious options. You can find a hundred and one varieties of Christianity, anything to suit your taste—classical Christianity, country Christianity, crunchy Christianity, be-bop Christianity and hip-hop Christianity. And that's not even to mention the hundreds of NRMs—New Religious Movements—invented every year in this country. Our culture wants to persuade us to just accept it all: let a thousand flowers bloom. Celebrate the diversity and richness and variety of American religious life. Above all, make no judgments. Don't examine, test, judge. That is the main thing the first Amendment prohibits, which, freely paraphrased, says "Thou shalt not test the spirits."

It goes against the cultural grain, but John says that we have to judge. Don't jump on every religious bandwagon that comes along. Don't believe every spirit, or everyone who claims to be a prophet. Pause. Stop. Take time to test the spirit. Ask whether the prophecies have come true. Ask whether the prophet or new movement is confessing Jesus in the flesh and all that this implies. Ask to whom they are listening, and who is listening to them. As John Stott says on this passage, *un*belief is a mark of spiritual maturity.

Any time we talk about spiritual warfare, or Satan, or false prophets, or antichrist, a tremble of terror runs through us. We think of horror movies where Satan is virtually all-powerful, where demons are relentless and blood-thirsty and surprising, the stuff of nightmares. That is not John's point in bringing all this up. John is not telling us ghost stories to scare us. There are evil spirits, the spirit of antichrist, in the world. There are false prophets, and they may even appear to succeed for a time. Yet John is perfectly confident, bold in his certainty about the outcome of this war. They are from the world, and the world listens to them, but even if they gain the whole world, we have nothing to fear. We are from God, and because of that we have overcome them. Not only that: we are from God, and the triumphant One is "in" us. We are confident of overcoming the world, of beating the world and all its spirits and all its terrors, because of the one who is among us as the body of

Christ, the one who is in each of us who is a member of that body. Don't be afraid of false teachers. Don't get anxious. There is no doubt about the outcome of this war of spirits. False prophets and false teachers speak from and to the world, but Christians have overcome the world, because the Spirit who is in them is greater than the spirit who is in the world.

9

GOD IS LOVE
1 John 4:7–5:5

Though I speak with the tongues of men and of angels, but have not love, I have become sounding brass or a clanging cymbal. And though I have the gift of prophecy, and understand all mysteries and all knowledge, and though I have all faith, so that I could remove mountains, but have not love, I am nothing. And though I bestow all my goods to feed the poor, and though I give my body to be burned, but have not love, it profits me nothing. Love suffers long and is kind; love does not envy; love does not parade itself, is not puffed up; does not behave rudely, does not seek its own, is not provoked, thinks no evil; does not rejoice in iniquity, but rejoices in the truth; bears all things, believes all things, hopes all things, endures all things. Love never fails. But whether there are prophecies, they will fail; whether there are tongues, they will cease; whether there is knowledge, it will vanish away. For we know in part and we prophesy in part. But when that which is perfect has come, then that which is in part will be done away. When I was a child, I spoke as a child, I understood as a child, I thought as a child; but when I became a man, I put away childish things. For now we see in a mirror, dimly, but then face to face. Now I know in part, but then I shall know just as I also am known. And now abide faith, hope, love, these three; but the greatest of these is love.

Thus far Paul, writing in 1 Corinthians, in what is undoubtedly the Bible's most famous passage on love. 1 John 4 rivals it. It is the great passage on love from the apostle who is most readily identified with this theme.

Through the first three chapters of his letter, John frequently exhorts his readers to love one another. Love is the difference between darkness and light. "The one who loves his brother abides in the light and there is no cause for stumbling in him," he writes, but "the one who hates his brother is in the darkness and walks in the darkness and does not know where he is going because the darkness has blinded his eyes" (2:10). Love is the difference between God and the devil. John says that the children of God and the children of the devil are known by their actions. God's children do righteousness, and the children of the devil do not, and righteousness is defined in terms of loving one's brother (3:10). God's commandment is that we trust in the name of Jesus and love one another (3:23). John also speaks of God's love for us: "See how great a love the Father has bestowed upon us, that we should be called the children of God; and such we are" (3:1). This is a constant theme throughout John's gospel as well.

Here in chapter 4, he brings it all together. The noun or verb "love" is used twenty-seven times (three times three times three) in 4:7–21, and twice more he addresses his readers as "beloved" (*agapātoi*, vv. 7, 11), which in Greek, as in English, contains the word "love." More than that, he connects all the aspects of love in a single intricate knot. He exhorts us to love. He describes the love of God displayed in Jesus. But he goes even further than Paul in grounding the commandment to love one another in the nature of God, the reality that "God is love." These aspects of love are all drawn together here in a way that is not found anywhere else in the Bible.

LOVE ONE ANOTHER

1 John 4:7Beloved, let us love one another, for love is from God, and whoever loves has been born of God and knows God. 8Anyone who does not love does not know God, because God is love. 9In this the love of God was made manifest among us, that God sent his only Son into the world, so that we might live through him. 10In this is love, not that we have loved God but that he loved us and sent his Son to be the propitiation for our sins. 11Beloved, if God so loved us, we also ought to love one another. 12No one has ever seen God; if we love one another, God abides in us and his love is perfected in us.

13By this we know that we abide in him and he in us, because he has given us of his Spirit. 14And we have seen and testify that the Father has sent his Son to be the Savior of the world. 15Whoever confesses that Jesus is the Son of God, God abides in him, and he in God. 16So we have come to know and to believe the love that God has for us. God is love, and whoever abides in love abides in God, and God abides in him. 17By this is love perfected with us, so that we may have confidence for the day of judgment, because as he is so also are we in this world. 18There is no fear in love, but perfect love casts out fear. For fear has to do with punishment, and whoever fears has not been perfected in love. 19We love because he first loved us. 20If anyone says, "I love God," and hates his brother, he is a liar; for he who does not love his brother whom he has seen cannot love God whom he has not seen. 21And this commandment we have from him: whoever loves God must also love his brother.

5:1Everyone who believes that Jesus is the Christ has been born of God, and everyone who loves the Father loves whoever has been born of him. 2By this we know that we love the children of God, when we love God and obey his commandments. 3For this is the love of God, that we keep his commandments. And his commandments are not burdensome. 4For everyone who has been born of God overcomes the world. And this is the victory that has overcome the world—our faith. 5Who is it that overcomes the world except the one who believes that Jesus is the Son of God?

Verses 7–11 are arranged in a complex chiastic structure (in this case, ABB'A'):

    A. Love one another
      B. a) Love is from God
          b) Everyone who loves
             c) Born of God and knows God
          b') Whoever does not love
          c')Does not know God
      a')God is love
      B' a) Love God manifested
          b) God sent Son
             c) So we might live
        a') In this is love
          b') Not that we loved God, but God loved us and sent Son
          c') To be propitiation for sins
    A' Love one another

The following section is also chiastic:

    A. No one beheld God, 12a
      B. Mutual love, God abides, love perfected, 12b
        C. Abiding in God, He in us, 13
          D. Bear witness to the Savior, 14
          D' Confessing that Jesus is Son, 15a
        C' God abides in him, he in us, 15b
      B' God's love for us, abiding in God, love perfected, 16–17a
    A' As He is, we are in the world, 17b

At the same time, another structure overlaps and intertwines another:

    A. God's love for us, 16
      B. Love perfected, 17a
        C. Confidence in judgment, 17b
          D. As He is, we are in the world, 17c
        C' No fear in love, 18a
        B' Perfect love casts out fear, 18b
    A' We love before He loved us, 19

These intertwined chiasms are framed by verses 12 and 20: "No one has beheld God" is answered by verse 20: "the one who does not love his brother whom he has seen cannot love God whom he has not seen." So, verses 12–20 (and perhaps 21) form a larger unit within interlocking chiasms between. This structure reinforces the great theme of the whole passage. A and A' in the first chiasm (12a and 17b) intriguingly match God's invisibility with the fact that we are "as He is" in the world, and the importance of this theme is highlighted by the fact that 17b (C) is also the center of the second chiasm. No one has seen God, and our love for God is visible in our love for the brothers. "We" are in the world what God is. The "problem" of God's invisibility is answered by our mutual love. The Word has manifested himself in flesh (1:1–4; 4:14), and by our union with the Word-made-flesh we are the visibility of the invisible God. Specifically, the invisible God who is love manifests himself in Jesus and in the love of the body of Christ. The God who is love is no longer seen and touched; but his love is visible, tangible, and audible in the love of his church.

Even this does not exhaust the structural complexity of the passage. The opening verses of chapter 5 share a number of terms and themes with 4:6–21. Verses 4:7 and 5:1–2 use the phrase "born of God" and the word "know," and 5:4 again speaks of being "born of God." To the twenty-seven uses of the word love (the verb *agapaō* or the noun *agapē*) found in chapter 4, verses 5:1–3 add five more, bringing the total to thirty-two (eight times four; eight for the first day of the new week, four signifying four corners). After verse 5:3, neither the noun nor the verb is used again in the letter. It is reasonable, then, to consider 4:7–5:5 a large unit of the letter, and the internal structure of the passage supports this conclusion.

> A. Beloved, love one another, for God is love, 4:7–10
> B. Beloved, no one has seen God, perfected love, 4:11–12
>   C. Abiding in God, abiding in love, 4:13–16
> B' Perfected love; no one has seen God, 4:17–21
> A' Those born of God believe and love, 5:1–5

One of the results of this arrangement is that verses 4:7–5:5 neatly match the second section of the letter, verses 1:5–2:17. Walking in darkness or light has to do with love of brothers (2:11), and the victory that John proclaims over the world and the evil one (2:12–14) matches the promise that our faith is the victory gaining victory over the world (5:4; the Greek is *hē nikē hē nikēsasa*).

LOVE ONE ANOTHER

John begins by exhorting his readers to love one another, and roots this in the fact that love has its source in God. Love—genuine love—comes from God (v. 7). On the other hand, John says starkly that the one who does not love does not know God (v. 8) and is not born of God. Love is the necessary fruit of knowing God. The only way to be genuinely loving, to act and live in real love, is to know God. Love is an essential fruit of knowing God, a *sine qua non* of Christian life.

This isn't designed to shake our assurance and confidence that we are born of God. John addresses his readers and us as ones who are loved by God: "God loved us," he says in verse 10, and again in verse 11 he repeats "God loved us." John doesn't hedge here. He doesn't say "God might or might not have loved us, or he loves some of us, or he loves the really spiritual ones among us." Speaking to the members of the church, John says bluntly and straight-forwardly, "God loved us." I examine the reasons for that assurance below, but we should note for now that John assumes his readers are beloved ones in the Beloved One. John doesn't want to snuff out a smoking reed or break a weak straw, though he certainly does want to snuff out false self-confidence. He doesn't want to undermine the confidence of the loving; he certainly wants to destroy the confidence of the loveless.

As he has been before, he is very blunt: the one who does not love does not know God. Earlier, he claimed that the one who hates his brother is a murderer, like Cain, a child of the devil, a part of the world. Love is not optional for believers. Love is the sign that we genuinely know God. If we can't get along with anyone, if we go from one fight to another, if we hate our wife or husband, our children, other Christians, we are not born of God. It's that simple. Love, further, is not just an attitude or emotion. Love takes action, and it takes the kind of action that Jesus took. Haters kill their brothers; lovers lay down their lives for their brothers. Remember Paul's words: "Love suffers long and is kind; love does not envy; love does not parade itself, is not puffed up; does not behave rudely, does not seek its own, is not provoked, thinks no evil; does not rejoice in iniquity, but rejoices in the truth; bears all things, believes all things, hopes all things, endures all things." Of course, we all sin; we are all loveless in one circumstance or another. But those necessary qualifications cannot be allowed to nullify what the Bible says: if Paul does not in some real way describe *you*, then the love of God doesn't abide in you. You are not born of God; you do not know God. It really is that simple.

Or think about this one: Paul says that love "does not seek its own." That is, love doesn't simply watch out for its own interests, and doesn't seek to force its own way. Love looks out for the interests of others. Today, our cultural flow encourages you to look out for Number One, to promote yourself, to grab for it, because you deserve it. Cultural flow flatters you, puffs you up with your own importance. Media and advertising tempt you to think it's all there for *you*. If you go with the cultural flow, however, you can't know God. It really is that simple.

The reason John gives for saying that the one who does not love is not born of God is a deep, deep theological reason. Knowing God produces love because love is an outflow of God's own inner character. God is love, and everyone who is "born of God" in the resurrection of Jesus bears a family resemblance to him (vv. 7–8). The one who knows God becomes like him, and God is love.

John's confession that God is love is one of the distinctive truths of Christian faith, and this is part of what Williams James might have called the "cash value" of the doctrine of the Trinity. In the modern world, the confession that God is triune has often been dismissed as pointless. What possible difference could it make that

God is three and one? It's a logical contradiction, and it's a logical contradiction that has no cash value, no practical import.

Nothing could be further from the truth, as Christians are discovering more and more in recent times. To say that God is love assumes that God is triune. God can be love only because he is plural, only because he is three, Father, Son, and Spirit. As theologians from Augustine through Richard of St. Victor to Karl Barth have said, to be genuine love, love requires an object, a beloved, an "other." Love is love only if it is directed out, only if it seeks the good of another. Self-love is not fully love. A lonely single person cannot be love. Allah cannot *be* love. Neither can the deist God of the eighteenth century, whom many Christians have confused with the God revealed in Jesus and the Bible. The pantheistic God of New Age ecological idolatry cannot be love, because everything is really him, so loving anything is loving him/it/herself. These gods, these idols, cannot *be* love, and they cannot express love for us. Their love for us cannot express their deepest inner being.

The true God, the living God, the God revealed in Jesus and in the Scriptures, *is* love. The true God lives in an eternal communion of perfect love and joy and peace, the Father loving the Son through the Spirit, and the Son returning love to the Father in the same Spirit. Because he is eternally and essentially love, he can love us with an eternal love. His love for us is the expression of his deepest character. God is not playing a role when he acts as our Father, our loving Bridegroom, the Spirit who is love. God is not adopting a pose or pretending. When God displays love, he displays himself. God loves others — creatures — because he has eternally loved others; the Father loves us as his children because he has eternally loved a Son in the Spirit. The Son loves us as brothers because he has eternally loved his Father in the Spirit. The Spirit loves us because he has eternally been the bond of love between Father and Son. Loving another was not a new experience when God created the world. It's an extension of the love that Father, Son, and Spirit have always had for one another.

We have to be careful here. Saying God is love is not quite the same as saying love is God. It is certainly not the same as saying that everything we *call* love is God. We can't draw from this the conclusion that loving homosexual relations are of God, or infer that fornication or adultery are from God so long as they are pursued in love. "God is love" does not mean that every "affection" is a sign of being born of God. Our affections and loves are often deeply perverted. We can "love" in all kinds of wicked ways. Every act of genuine love comes from God, but not everything we want to call love comes from God.

MANIFEST LOVE

For John, this eternal and essential love of God is manifested in God's actions, specifically in the fact that God the Father sent the Son to give us life (v. 9, 14). John clearly has the whole career of Jesus in view, not simply the incarnation. He refers specifically to Jesus' propitiating death (v. 10), and no doubt has the resurrection in mind as well. God's love is displayed in the whole career of Jesus.

John's emphasis on the manifestation of God's love in Jesus highlights the reasons for digressing about love in a letter addressing the Judaizing crisis of the early church. Judaizers refuse to love because they maintain barriers that Jesus broke down; in effect, they refuse to acknowledge that God is love. A god who remains hidden away forever is not a god of love who flows out in sacrificial love for his creatures. A god who refuses to come in tangible, visible flesh is not a god of love. The god of the Judaizers is the remote god, the aloof god, the god approached only by the gnostic (or Jewish) elite. He is not a god of love, much less a god of manifest love.

John insists on several points. First, John highlights the priority of God's love over our love for him. Love is not defined, or initiated, by our act of loving God, but rather by his loving us (v. 10). As John says later, we love him in response to his prior love (v. 19). He is the Bridegroom whose passion awakens the love of the Bride. There is an "ought" here. Verse 11 says that God's love produces an obligation in us. Since he loved us, we *ought* to love him and one another. At another level, love and the response of love are naturally, inevitably connected. God loves us, and the magnetic attraction of his love awakens love in us.

The same dynamic works in human experience as well. If someone loves us, that creates an obligation on our part. We ought to love those who love us; if we hate those who do good to us, we are ungrateful wretches. In addition, love arouses the response of love. You want your children to respond obediently to you, and they ought to. You've given them many things, you've loved them, and they ought to love you in response. But this happens in practice only if that "ought" is inspired by your love for them. God inspires loving obedience in us through his manifest love for us in Jesus, not by browbeating and issuing orders. There is a place for orders, but orders will not be obeyed, or they will at most be obeyed reluctantly, outside a context of love. You want your children to obey you? Give yourself to them in order to inspire their love.

The reason this works is because God's love sets the pattern for ours, and that means that we are called to give ourselves for one another as God gave himself for us (v. 11). This gives us a specific idea of what love looks like: it looks like Jesus. This helps us, once again, to see that discernment and love are friends, not enemies; partners, not competitors. Jesus discerns the evil motives of his enemies, and he strongly rebukes them. But he does all he does out of love. He rebukes his opponents in order to deliver them from their self-delusions and errors. He challenges them in order to liberate them from the spirit of error. This is love in action, love that loves enough to challenge the wickedness of the one it loves. Jesus' love is also self-giving. He had no need to come to be the propitiation for our sin. He gave himself freely for our sake, because he loves us in spite of our sins and rebellions and resistances.

John insists that the incarnation, ministry, and death of Jesus are not some bizarre contradiction of God's character. It's not as if God-in-himself is surly and unforgiving, while God-in-his-revelation is loving and kind. The incarnation, the life of Jesus, the death of Jesus, the resurrection of Jesus—they are all manifestations or revelations of God's character. Note the sequence in verses 8 and 9: God is love, and God manifested his love in sending the Son. We should also notice here that the incarnation is a manifestation not only of the love of Jesus but of the love of "God" (v. 9), a reference to the sending Father. We sometimes get the idea that there is an inner contradiction in God, that the Father is a somewhat cold, distant, authoritarian figure, who needs to be won over by the kind and loving Jesus. As we saw above, God's wrath does need to be appeased, but the apostles insist that the Son comes as an expression of the Father's love.

You want to know what God is like, really? Take a look at the gospel. If you have seen Jesus, if you have seen him in the manger, seen him tempted in the wilderness, seen him passionately fighting the Pharisees who oppress his people, freely offering himself on the cross, powerfully rising again from the dead—when you have seen all this, you have seen God who is love. Jesus did all this out of love for us, and because his Father sent him out of love. You want to see the love of God, read about Jesus. For whoever has seen Jesus has seen the Father.

ATHEISM

From about 500 AD to 1500 AD, atheism in our sense—the denial of the existence of any god whatever—was virtually unthinkable. It was an uncanny aberration. It's not that the charge of atheism was unknown. The charge was made against the early Christians, and made by early Christians against others. Because Christians rejected the traditional deities of the Roman world, they were accused of being atheists—as well as being cannibalistic and incestuous. And they accepted that label, insofar as it applied to false gods. Justin the Martyr said that "[w]e do proclaim ourselves atheists as regards those whom you call gods, but not with respect to the Most True God." Jews and Christians were the first atheists— the first to deny divine character to the proliferating deities of the world. Had the Romans had their way, they would have been happy to proclaim Jesus a god, which would have meant he was a god on par with Zeus and Athena and all the others. Christians were atheists in denying the realities and divinity of these gods.

For ancients, atheism usually meant being ungodly. That is the charge against Christians. Justin was willing to level the charge of atheism against others, but what he had in mind was practical atheism: "Before God no man has an excuse if he does evil, for all men have been created with the power to reason and to reflect. If anyone does not believe that God has an interest in these [virtue and vice], he will by some artifice imply either that God does not exist . . . or that He is [as unmoved] as a stone [by human actions]."[1] In order to deflect the possibility of being judged for their sins, sinners denied the existence of the specific God who was supposed to act as their judge. If we pretend he doesn't exist, maybe nothing will happen.

Beginning in the sixteenth century, what we know now as atheism became increasingly widespread. Even at this time, the term didn't always mean what it means for us. Luther, Calvin, Zwingli, and Erasmus were charged with atheism by their opponents, and they were all not only believers in God but believers in the Triune God. The word "atheist" could be used simply for rhetorical purposes, a "kind of obscenity meant to cause a shudder in the audience of the faithful."[2] Over the following centuries, disbelief in gods of all kinds became increasingly common. The United States lagged behind, but by the end of the nineteenth century atheism became a culturally viable option.

At the same time, the practical atheism that Justin condemned became the leading feature of modern culture. Modernity is a civilization organized to exclude God from everyday public life. Modern politicians invoke God, but their day-to-day policymaking assumes that God has nothing specific to say to politics. No one turns to Moses or Jesus when he is deciding how to revise the tax code. Sellers might employ religious imagery to sell their products, but our economy is organized on the assumption that economic life

1. Quoted in Alan Kors on *Atheism in France: The Orthodox Sources of Disbelief* (Princeton, 1990).
2. Lucien Fevre, *The Problem of Unbelief in the Sixteenth Century* (Harvard, 1982).

is autonomous, that God, if he exists, is worried about more important things than our checkbooks and portfolios. Our public schools teach children implicitly, if not explicitly, that God and his Word are irrelevant to learning. They simply ignore God, in the name of the First Amendment.

Now, how did this come about? How did atheism become a cultural option? How did practical atheism become the dominant flavor of our civilization? There are no doubt many explanations for this, but John offers a crucial insight. Because of the way he links the availability of God—his visibility, his knowability—to love, we might say God's *believability* depends directly on the way Christians behave toward one another.

SEEING GOD

John says that no one has seen God (v. 12), yet he begins his letter by emphasizing how the apostles saw the "Word of Life" (1:1–3). The Word that is God (John 1:1) makes himself visible and tangible by manifesting himself in the flesh. God is unseen in himself, and we can't invent instruments that will enable us to see him. If God is going to be seen, he must reveal himself. In his gospel, John proclaims that this is precisely what God has done through Jesus. No one has seen God at any time, he says in the first chapter of his gospel, but then he goes on to say that the only-begotten Son has "exegeted" the Father. And Jesus says, in response to a question from Philip about seeing the Father, "Whoever has seen Me has seen the Father" (John 14:9). God the Father has revealed his character in his image—his Son. If you want to know what God is like, look at Jesus. There is no God lurking "behind" the gospel. The gospel reveals the righteousness, love, mercy, and goodness of God. They are all seen in the fact of the incarnation and the specific works that Jesus did in his life. When God came out of hiding, he showed himself as he really is.

The Son was sent to be savior of the world (1 John 4:14), and it's only as the only-begotten Son that he can be Savior. This is true in the usual sense that Jesus is the "contact point" between God and man, though it's also true in a more subtle sense. Jesus saves us by communicating life (1 John 4:9), but is life something that can be communicated? Is life something that can flow out from the Father? Is life something that can be shared? For trinitarian Christians, the answer is a "duh": life always has been shared, because the Father has never been without his Son; the life of the Father has always been shared with his Son. Life can be distributed to creation only because there is an only-begotten Son.

However, now *Jesus* has disappeared. He is now invisible too. And what are we left with? 1 John 1 says that we are left with the eyewitness testimony of the apostles. They have seen, heard, and touched, and now declare to us *what* they have seen and heard and touched. In order to have fellowship with the unseen Father and his ascended Son, one has to have fellowship with the apostles. But now they are gone too. We can't consult John and his eyewitness. We can't interview Peter. How do we have fellowship with the apostles, who had fellowship with the Word of Life manifested in flesh? We have it through the testimony in Scripture, but here John goes beyond that and says that we have a living image of the God who is love. God makes himself visible and available in the world through *us*.

Though God is unseen, he still manifests himself in flesh, in the flesh that makes up the body of Christ, the flesh of our brothers and sisters. That's why John moves from saying "no one has beheld God" to saying "if we love one another" (v. 12). That's why he ends one section of the passage by saying that no one can love the unseen God unless he loves his visible brothers (v. 20). Loving the brothers is a primary way of loving God. More dramatically, the love that is God becomes incarnate in Jesus first of all, and secondarily in the love of Christians for one another: "As He is, so also are we in this world" (v. 17). In other words, John places on us the burden of showing God: the world knows the God who is love through the love we have for one another.

This is, in a sense, nothing new for humanity. It was Adam's original calling. Adam was created as the image of the invisible God. The word "image" in Genesis 1 is the same as the word for "graven images" elsewhere in the Bible, and there is an analogy in the uses. Baal was not directly visible, but he manifested himself, and claimed his rights as a god, by having an image set up in the temple. The image of Baal was the visibility of Baal; it was not identical to Baal himself, but it was a sign of his dominion and his presence with his worshipers. The image asserted Baal's claim on the world. Adam was created as God's image in that sense. Adam was created to be the visibility of God in the world, manifesting the presence of the invisible God. Through Adam's visible presence, the dominion of the invisible God was evident. Adam sinned, and therefore there was a disjunction between the original and the copy; the original—God—was no longer clearly visible in the image. Through Christ, who is the image of God in the fullest sense, this is restored. When the Son assumed human flesh, he re-imprinted the divine image on humanity. Those who are in Christ are re-conformed to their archetype and model, becoming sons in the Son.[3] The church as the new humanity is now fulfilling the calling originally placed on Adam to image God in the creation. We are the visibility of the invisible God in the world.

Now, we should keep this in mind as we think about the rise of atheism in the modern world. At the same time that atheism was rising, the church was breaking into (sometimes literally) warring camps. For the past several centuries, we have continued in war. Not all division and conflict is bad, and some of the divisions within the church have been necessary. A great deal, however, has been sinful and unloving. Christians hate one another groundlessly. If we are the visibility of God in the world, if God's believability depends on us, is it any wonder that atheism arose in the age when Christians began killing each other? If our love is the visibility of the God who is love, how is anyone to know God when we hate one another?

---

3. This is a crucial part of the Christology of Maximus the Confessor, as explained by John Meyendorff, *Christ in Eastern Christian Thought* (Crestwood, NY: St. Vladimir's Seminary, 1979).

RENEWING LOVE

How do we go about re-establishing the love we should have for one another? This is an essential part of achieving Christian mission. How do we do it? It isn't done by self-exertions, resolutions, or teeth-gritted determination to be loving. It comes by contact with the source of love, the God who is love. It comes through what John calls abiding in God.

John brings up this image of abiding or dwelling in God in his gospel. There, he records Jesus saying that he and the Father dwell in each other (17:20–23):

> I do not ask on behalf of these alone, but for those also who believe in Me through their word; that they may all be one; even as You, Father, are in Me and I in You, that they also may be in Us, so that the world may believe that You sent Me. The glory which You have given Me I have given to them, that they may be one, just as We are one; I in them and You in Me, that they may be perfected in unity, so that the world may know that You sent Me, and loved them, even as You have loved Me.

Jesus speaks of a mutual abiding of Father and Son in one another. The Son is the Father's dwelling-place, and the Father is the Son's dwelling place. The Father dwells in the Son through the Spirit, and the Son dwells in the Father through the Spirit. They abide in one another, live in one another, in an eternal fellowship of loving communion. That is the life of God.

The main thrust of the prayer is that the disciples would be grafted into the mutual communion of Father and Son. He prays that he would be in the disciples, and that the Father would be in him, so that "they may be in us," the disciples dwelling in, abiding in, sharing in, the communion and love of the Father and the Son. That's what John is saying here again in his epistle: when we love one another, we are participating in the mutual loving-indwelling of the Father and Son (vv. 12, 16). We know that this mutual indwelling is real because of the work of the Spirit (v. 13), who witnesses that God dwells in us and we in him.

More, the Spirit is the agent of our communion with God: the Spirit who searches the deep things of God, the Spirit who is the bond of love between Father and Son, dwells in us, so that through the Spirit God abides in us and through the Spirit we abide in him. In us, his love is brought to completion, to maturity (v. 12). The love that we have for one another comes from abiding in the Triune God who lives in an eternal fellowship of love.

One result of abiding in love and abiding in God is that we are delivered from fear in judgment (v. 17). Scripture frequently encourages us to fear God, and fear is not just an Old Testament virtue. We know Proverbs says that the fear of the Lord is the beginning of wisdom. 2 Corinthians 7:1 also speaks of godly fear: "Therefore, having these promises, beloved, let us cleanse ourselves from all filthiness of the flesh and spirit, perfecting holiness in the fear of God." Ephesians 5:17–21 echoes this theme.

> Therefore do not be unwise, but understand what the will of the Lord is. And do not be drunk with wine, in which is dissipation; but be filled with the Spirit, speaking to one another in psalms and hymns and spiritual songs, singing and making melody in your heart to the Lord, giving thanks always for all things to God the Father in the name of our Lord Jesus Christ, submitting to one another in the fear of God.

John is not contradicting the rest of Scripture when he says that perfected love dispels fear. He assumes, with the rest of Scripture, that there are different sorts of fear. We have a right fear of God if we are awed by his power and majesty. We have a right fear of God if our fear of God draws us close to him, to abide in him. We have a right fear of God when we honor him as our Maker, Lord, and Savior. John is talking about a cowering fear, the fear that God is out to get us, the anxious worry that we will not stand in judgment. John is talking about the fear of Adam, the fear that came from a bad conscience and drove Adam to hide in the garden. This kind of fear is driven out by the love that God has shown us (v. 19). Since God has given his Son, we have no reason to fear his punishments; he is our

Father, and if he disciplines us, it is for our salvation, not for punishment. This kind of fear is driven out as our love for one another matures: "Perfect love casts out fear" (v. 18).

We can put it this way: fear moves us, and the difference between right and wrong fear is the *direction* it moves us. Adam feared God, and hid in the garden. Wrong fear drives us away from God's presence. Right fear draws us closer, in awed fascination and quaking love toward the God who is a consuming fire. It's the fear we have when we see something so utterly fearsome that we just have to get a closer look. Again, Judaizers are in view: they don't have proper fear for God because their fear drives them away from God, away from the protected holy places and taboo objects. In the Son, God has appeared, and the right response is to fear and draw near, through the veil, into the presence of the glory.

John Stott notes that 1 John 4:19 indicates that the church's great characteristic is love, not fear. That is, it *should* be. Is it? Hardly. Read the next piece of direct mail you get from some Christian advocacy group. Look at the listings in a Christian book catalog or bookstore. Analyze the rhetoric of your favorite Christian political figure. Read some of the web punditry about Barack Obama. Think of the conspiracy-mongering that gets mixed up with Christianity in many circles. How many dozens of Christian ministries continue to exist only because of the fear they are able to generate? As Jesus didn't say: you can tell a Christian by his fear.

Unfortunately, the experience of many Christians is Adamic fear rather than the attractive fear of fascination. Many Christians describe their own experience with God as an experience of constant fear of punishment. Many Christians believe that being a Christian is a matter of keeping the rules, and that God is waiting up in heaven to zap anyone who commits the least infraction against the rules. Many Christians experience God as a slavemaster, rather than a liberator from slavery. How does this happen?

Some of it is certainly distorted doctrine and teaching in the church. Some of it is a failure to embody the gospel in the Lord's Table. Much of it, I suspect, has to do with our conduct as parents. What kind of portrait of God does our parenting portray before our children? Fathers, ask yourself: if your children's first notion of fatherhood comes from you, what connotations will come to mind when you call God "Father"? In any case, this service—this abject fear, this fear of punishment—is precisely what John says the gospel removes. God loves us, he's demonstrated his love to us in his Son. And the more this gospel grips our hearts, the more that love will be visible in our love for one another.

FATHER AND SON(S)

"Now abide faith, hope, and love, these three. But the greatest of these is love." That's how Paul concludes his great chapter on love, and John does something similar here at the end of the great section on love in his first epistle. Here John not only concludes his teaching on love, but he shows the relationship between love and faith and love and hope, though he names "hope" with the word "victory." John as much as Paul could have said: "Now abide faith, hope, and love, these three."

John has already said that love for the brothers is a sign of being born of God (4:7), and here he adds that believing Jesus is the Messiah and Son of God is another sign of being born, or begotten, of God (5:1, 5). Faith and love are inseparable, as verse 1 indicates. The first part says that the one who believes in Jesus is begotten of God, and John moves immediately from talking about faith to talking about love. The last line of verse 1 literally reads, "Whoever loves the one who begets loves the one begotten." Believing in Jesus as the Christ is a sign of being begotten, and loving the begotten children is a sign that one loves the father. A child who loves his parents will also love his siblings.

John has written similar things earlier in the letter, but he shifts the language here in a couple of ways that highlight different aspects of his message. The word translated "born" in verse 1b is "begotten" (*gennaō*); it is related to the word he uses in his gospel to describe Jesus as the "Only-Begotten" son. Elsewhere, John emphasizes the uniqueness of the Son's relationship with the Father, but he emphasizes the continuity between the "Only-begotten" Son and the many "sons" who are also "begotten" of God. In and through the work of the Only-Begotten, we all are begotten of God.

As I have suggested earlier, the specific event John seems to have in mind is the resurrection. Elsewhere in the New Testament, Psalm 2 is quoted in contexts where it refers to the resurrection (Acts 13:33). Jesus is the eternally begotten Son, but he is begotten in time by being raised from the dead. When we come to share in that resurrection by faith in Jesus as the Christ, we also are "begotten" of him. We are begotten from the dead in Jesus, the firstborn of the resurrection.

Intriguingly, John shifts the direction of his argument here. In earlier chapters, John has said that being born of God expresses itself in love for the brothers. Our love for one another is the sign of our love for God: whoever hates his brother cannot love God. Here, John reverses that statement. Our love for the Father, not our love for the brothers, is the sign of being born of God (v. 1). As Brown says, "One tests love for God by love for the brothers (4:20–21) and then tests love for brothers by love for God."[4] Both are true, and exist in a circular relationship. When we're born of God, we love the brothers and we love God; we love the brothers as an expression of our love for God, and love God in loving our brothers.

This has important implications not only for the family of God, the church, but for our natural families. John states it as a kind of axiom that one cannot love the begetter without loving the begotten; one cannot love the father without loving the children who bear a resemblance to their father. There are families where the children claim to have a deep affection for their parents but can't stand to be around one another. That is perverse, John says. If we can't love those who are stamped with the image of the father, we can't possibly love the father either. But it works the other way too: you can't love the siblings, the brothers, without loving the father. Some families are divided by generation, where the children main-

---

4. Brown, *The Epistles of John* (Anchor Bible; Garden City: Doubleday, 1985), 566.

tain close contact and fellowship but plot and scheme together in defiance of their parents. They try to love the begotten without loving the begetter. John says this is perverse too.

John is also saying that the opponents he faces are incapable of loving God or loving brothers. According to Brown, those who have left the church and don't confess Jesus as the Christ don't have any brothers to love. The members of the church are only brothers insofar as they are children of God, and they are children of God only insofar as they believe in the Eternal Son of God, come in flesh, Jesus. If they don't believe in and confess Jesus as Son and Messiah, they have no brotherhood together, no common nature.[5]

According to liberal theology and political theory, we can all get along based on our common share in original, Adamic humanity. We are all human beings, with human rights, and we can live in harmony and love without any appeal to Jesus or the gospel. This liberalism is impossible without the influence of the gospel. Prior to the penetration of the gospel, dominant groups often didn't consider people outside their group to be fully human. There were Greeks, and there were barbarians, little better than beasts; there were freemen and there were slaves. Liberalism assumes the Christian view that there is one creator of all men, and that God has made of one blood all nations.

However, this liberal notion of human equality is unsustainable without belief in Jesus. Look at the world around us. If we factor out God as creator of all men, and Jesus as the one in whom men are brothers, what basis is there for saying that we are all in the same boat, all members of the same common humanity? The last one hundred years, during which liberalism triumphed, has seen as much war and slaughter as any century in history. At the same time that liberalism proclaimed the gospel of the Brotherhood of Man without God, one group was busy slaughtering another—or defective members of their own group—by the millions; corpses piled up in the former Soviet Union, China, Cambodia, Nazi Ger-

---

5. Brown, *Epistles*, 566.

many, Uganda. Adamic humanity is divided, at war with itself. Adam's first son, after all, was Cain, and Cainites have continued to murder and maim for the last six thousand years.

If there is to be unity and harmony among peoples and races and tongues and tribes, there must be something *other* than the common Adamic humanity, the common humanity that migrated from Babel. There has to be a *new* Adamic humanity, confessing that Jesus is begotten of the Father, and welcoming as brothers all who profess Jesus and all who are begotten of the same Father. Without that Christological confession, there is no basis for unity of the race. The Fatherhood of God and the brotherhood of man are insufficient for harmony among peoples. What we need is both the Fatherhood of God and the Brotherhood of *God*, human beings united not only by a common Father but in their elder Brother, the incarnate Son.

John also implies that his opponents are incapable of love because loving God means keeping his commandments. I've argued throughout this commentary that John is dealing mainly with Judaizers and Jews. It may seem odd to charge Jews with a failure to keep the commandments of God, but that's exactly what Jesus repeatedly says about the Jews. They replace the commandments of God with their own traditions, and pile burdens on the backs of Jews, as Pharaoh piled up burdens on Israel in Egypt. The Pharisees want their fellow Jews to make bricks without straw, and Jesus, the Greater Moses, comes to break the yoke of oppression. Jesus says that they keep the small laws in order to justify their disobedience to the big laws. They tithe on their seeds, but they neglect the whole purpose of the law—mercy, justice, and truth.

John describes love as a matter of doing God's commandments. For John, love and obedience are not opposites, but intimately connected. As Jesus said, "If you love me, you will keep my commandments" (John 14:15). John adds, as Jesus himself did, that his commandments are not burdensome (v. 5; cf. Matt. 11:30; 23:4). Jesus is our master, but he is a kind master who does not weigh us down.

This, of course, is quite opposed to much of what we find in Christianity—even evangelical and Reformed Christianity—today.

Law and gospel are set against each other. There is some truth to that in some contexts. We don't make ourselves acceptable to God by keeping the law, and the Torah as the system of worship and life that governed Israel did not bring salvation. When John talks about what it means to live the Christian life day-by-day, he describes it in terms of faith, love, and obedience to commandments. Without attention to God's commandments, love threatens to collapse into sentimentality and affirmation. On the other hand, if we keep God's commandments without love, without sincere desire for the good of our brothers, then we are also separating what God has joined together. Law should be infused with and motivated by love; love expresses itself in keeping commandments.

What does it mean to love a woman? Among other things, it means that you don't treat her as a sexual object and don't lust for her in your heart. In short, you love a sister, or co-worker, or female friend by keeping Jesus' prohibition of lust. What does it mean to love when you hear a rumor about a brother's sin? It means you don't become a tale-bearer; you confront him with his sin if that's necessary, but you don't spread rumors and gossip and slander. In short, you love your brother by keeping Jesus' commandments. What does it mean to love your employees if you own a business? The law says that employers are responsible to pay their employees, and not withhold their payment. The law says that employers should provide a day of "ceasing," a Sabbath day. Employers love their employees by keeping the commandments of Jesus.

VICTORY

The result of our faith and love, our love-in-faith and faith-in-love, is victory over the world (5:4–5). The world is organized around Cainite hatred, but we can be confident that our love will triumph. The world denies that Jesus is begotten of God, but we can be confident that eventually every knee will bow and every tongue confess Jesus as Lord. How does this work? How does our faith overcome the world?

First, notice that John is talking about victory, not endurance. The word overcome (*nikaō*) is built from the same root as the word victory in verse 4b: "This is the victory that gains the victory over the world, our faith." John doesn't want us to endure, survive, or slog on through. He says that we should triumph, and that our faith does triumph. Jesus doesn't want you to learn to live with your habitual sins; he wants you to triumph over them. Second, the faith that John talks about is very specific. It's not general faith in God, nor is it self-referential faith in faith. He's not talking about the strength of faith per se, or the importance of believing something, no matter what. John says that the faith that overcomes the world is belief that Jesus is the Christ and that Jesus is the Son of God.

Both of these are royal titles. Christ means Anointed One, and refers to Jesus as the one anointed with the Spirit as Priest, King, and Prophet. "Son of God" in the Bible refers to Adam, Israel, and to the Davidic king as the representative head of Israel. Here, it means confession that Jesus is King, the Lord of the world. The faith that overcomes the world is not faith in God in general. It's faith that Jesus is the Anointed King, the Son of God now installed at his Father's right hand, the King of kings and Lord of lords. If we believe this, we overcome the world.

Stephen Westerholm has put it this way: you've seen the movie dozens of times. The hero is captured by the villain, and the villain holds all the cards. The villain thinks he's triumphed, and he's likely to celebrate by monologing about the success of all his plans. If it's a melodrama, he'll rub his hands and lick his lips and spin the edges of his handlebar moustache in glee. But the hero knows something: he knows that the cavalry is on the way, or that he has already unloaded the villain's gun, or that there are even now friendly rats gnawing at his bonds. The villain knows none of this, and when the hero escapes and the villain is defeated, he'll say (if it's a melodrama), "Drat, foiled again!" That's the position of the Christian. The world may hate us. The world tells lies about us. The world attacks with all it has. But we know something they don't know. We know there are resources for triumph that they know nothing about, and we are confident that, be it late or soon, rescue will come. We know that there is a parousia coming, an appearance of our Emperor from heaven, and that gives us confidence (*parrēsia*).

Suppose it doesn't. Suppose the villain pulls the trigger of a *loaded* gun. Suppose the rats can't get through the ropes fast enough. Suppose the cavalry went in the wrong direction or got slowed down. Suppose we get to the cross or the scaffold and no one comes along to rescue us. What then? Where is the triumph there? This is where the specific faith that John talks about comes into play, because he's talking about faith in Christ, the Son of God, who was not only eternally begotten by the Father but begotten from the dead by the power of the Spirit. Jesus didn't triumph by escaping death, by pulling himself down from the cross. He didn't gain victory by running away when the soldiers came to Gethsemane. His victory gained the victory by triumphing over death. He gained the victory by being the firstborn from the dead.

This is the kind of "overcoming" that John has in mind when he uses the word in Revelation: "And they overcame him because of the blood of the Lamb and because of the word of their testimony, and they did not love their life even when faced with death" (12:11). They overcame *through* death, as Jesus did, because they knew that even when the villain pulled the trigger, or released the sharks, or lowered them into the boiling cauldron, triumph had already come and is still coming. Late or soon, it is coming.

This means that they can't do *anything* to harm us. Nothing. They've got *no* power over us. The world can do its worst, and they can't touch us. The world lies about us, but we know that Jesus is going to judge the world in the end and vindicate his people, stop the mouth of the accuser, reveal the truth. They can slaughter and kill, but eventually we'll come back, glorified, and even in history our death is the seed that goes into the ground and bears much fruit. They can stretch us out on the cross, but we have learned the secret of life—that the cross is the gateway to new life, that death will be swallowed up by victory, that Jesus has turned the tomb into a womb. Whatever might look like defeat, death, failure—*isn't*.

In Christ it never is, not forever, not for long. For this is the victory that gains victory over the world—our faith.

10

THE FATHER AND HIS SON(S)
1 John 5:6–21

Love is one of the central themes of 1 John, but as we saw in the last chapter, John is equally concerned, as Paul was, with the other two theological virtues, faith and hope. Several times, he encourages his readers to confidence and hope at the coming of the Lord (2:28; 3:3, 21; 4:17; 5:14) and he is as insistent as Paul on the necessity of faith. He uses the verb "believe" (*pisteuō*) ten times in the letter, half of which occur in the last section (5:10 [three times], 13 [twice]), and the adjective "faithful" (*pistos*) and noun "faith" (*pistis*) once each (1:9; 5:4, respectively). These twelve uses of the *pist*-group suggest a connection with the twelve tribes of Israel; the new Israel is marked by faith, specifically by faith in Jesus. Along with faith, the final section of 1 John emphasizes the testimony that supports faith. Of the seven uses of the verb "witness" (*martureō*) in the letter, five appear in 5:6–10, and the noun *marturia* occurs only in the final chapter, occurring six times in verses 9–11. One of the two others occurs in 1:2, thus framing the letter with references to apostolic and divine testimony (the other occurrence is in 4:14). Belief in the testimony concerning Jesus is necessary if the church is to be the community of love that John says it should be.

1 John 5:6–21 is itself framed by a set of repeated phrases and words. Verse 6 refers to the "one who came" (*ho elthōn*) and verse 20 specifies that the Son of God is the one who has come (*hēkei*). The Spirit who testifies to Jesus is the truth (vv. 6–7, *alētheia*) and verse 20 uses the adjective form of the same word three times (*alēthinon*). There may be a numerical connection as well: verse 8 speaks of three truthful witnesses, and verse 20 speaks three times of the God who is true. Within this frame, the section follows a roughly chiastic structure:

> A. God's true witness to the Son, 5:6–10
> > B. Life in the Son, 5:11–13
> > > C. Confidence in prayer, 5:14–15
> > > > D. Sins to death, 5:16–17
> > > C' Confidence against the evil one, 5:18–19
> > A' Son has come, knowing the one who is true, 5:20a
> > > B' True God and eternal life, 5:20b–21

TEXTUAL TRANSMISSION

1 John 5:6 This is he who came by water and blood—Jesus Christ; not by the water only but by the water and the blood. And the Spirit is the one who testifies, because the Spirit is the truth. 7For there are three that testify: 8the Spirit and the water and the blood; and these three agree. 9If we receive the testimony of men, the testimony of God is greater, for this is the testimony of God that he has borne concerning his Son. 10Whoever believes in the Son of God has the testimony in himself. Whoever does not believe God has made him a liar, because he has not believed in the testimony that God has borne concerning his Son. 11And this is the testimony, that God gave us eternal life, and this life is in his Son. 12Whoever has the Son has life; whoever does not have the Son of God does not have life.

¹³ I write these things to you who believe in the name of the Son of God that you may know that you have eternal life. ¹⁴ And this is the confidence that we have toward him, that if we ask anything according to his will he hears us. ¹⁵ And if we know that he hears us in whatever we ask, we know that we have the requests that we have asked of him.

¹⁶If anyone sees his brother committing a sin not leading to death, he shall ask, and God will give him life—to those who commit sins that do not lead to death. There is sin that leads to death; I do not say that one should pray for that. ¹⁷All wrongdoing is sin, but there is sin that does not lead to death.

¹⁸We know that everyone who has been born of God does not keep on sinning, but he who was born of God protects him, and the evil one does not touch him.

¹⁹We know that we are from God, and the whole world lies in the power of the evil one.

²⁰And we know that the Son of God has come and has given us understanding, so that we may know him who is true; and we are in him who is true, in his Son Jesus Christ. He is the true God and eternal life. ²¹Little children, keep yourselves from idols.

Some Bibles include the statement in verse 7 "there are three that bear witness in heaven: the Father, the Word, and the Holy Spirit, and these three are one." This translation moves directly from "there are three that bear witness" to "the Spirit and the water and the blood." The reason for this divergence is that Bible translators use different texts. The New Testament, of course, was originally written in Greek. The original documents of the New Testament, the actual parchments that John or one of his secretaries wrote out, don't exist anymore. What we have are hundreds of copies of the New Testament or fragmentary parts of the New Testament in Greek, as well as translations of the Greek New Testament into other languages, particularly Latin. And these various texts differ in various details.

The variations are often grammatical, such as a difference in verb tense. Sometimes the wording of various texts is slightly different, but without a change in content. In John 1:18, for instance, some manuscripts say that the "only-begotten *God* . . . has explained

Him," the Father. Other manuscripts say, "the only-begotten *Son* . . . has explained Him." The first text asserts the deity of Jesus more overtly, but there is nothing untrue about either reading.

1 John 5:7–8 is one of the most famous textual variations in the New Testament, and has a colorful history. The verse appears in the Latin Vulgate, and when Erasmus was publishing a Greek edition of the New Testament, he was asked if he was going to include it. He said he would, but he had no Greek texts that had the verse. Not long after that, someone produced a Greek text with the verse in it, so Erasmus put it into his edition. It is all too tidy. One cannot help but be suspicious that the Greek text was not found, but created out for this very purpose.

As a result, the evidence is strongly against this verse. No ancient Greek manuscript has the statement. Perhaps the strongest evidence against it being in the original text, or in old copies of 1 John, is the fact that none of the early Greek fathers cite it. They went through almost a century of debate about the deity of Christ, and the triune nature of God, and this verse would have served as a neat proof text for the Trinity. They scoured the New Testament for relevant passages, and sometimes used passages to defend the Trinity or the deity of Christ that seem quite a stretch. None of them quotes the disputed section of 1 John 5:7–8. The best explanation for this is that they didn't mention it because they didn't know about it.

Discussions like this can be unnerving. Evangelical Christians profess that the Bible is the Word of God, and we believe that it's the Word of God in a very specific way. It's not just the ideas or general teachings of the Bible that come from God, but the written text itself. That's what Paul says in 1 Timothy 3: the *Scripture*s are God-breathed, the written documents, the texts. We believe that these texts are reliable, without error, infallible, and inerrant. Then we learn that there is dispute about what the text *is*, and that text differs from text. How can we be confident that we have the Word of God at all? Why didn't God preserve the original writing of John on a magical parchment that never decays? Why didn't he put it on golden tablets so it wouldn't have to be copied out?

When we reflect on the questions, we discover that this is consistent with the way God always works. God didn't bypass time when he set out to redeem the world. He doesn't bypass the changes, the messiness, the complexity of actual human history. On the contrary, the God we worship works through history. He's in complete control of all the messiness, and what looks haphazard and problematic to us is actually the perfect expression of his purposes. History is not an obstacle to God revealing himself. History is the vehicle of his revelation to us. Similarly, the Scriptures that we have—with all the variants and all the necessity of judging what's in and what's not—is precisely the vehicle of revelation that God has given us. In the end, this means that trusting Scripture is an act of faith. It's not an act of blind faith. Faith isn't fantasy. Faith is trust in God when appearances suggest that he is not trustworthy. God has promised to guide us, to lead us by Word and Spirit. If he chooses to lead us with Greek texts that are not pristine, then we humbly trust that he knows what he is doing. We trust that he wants us to wrestle with his book, and grow up in the process.

WATER AND BLOOD

A number of typological echoes are in the background of John's reference to "water and blood." Among other things, he is reminding us of Passover and the exodus, specifically the blood of the Passover lamb, the water of the Red Sea, and the Spirit-cloud that led Israel through the wilderness. Jesus is the new Moses, leading a new Passover and exodus, his way marked by Spirit, water, and blood. Ultimately, John reaches back to the beginning of the Bible, where the first creation was the work of the Spirit who hovered over the water. Creation emerged by Spirit and water. But John adds a third term: blood. He's suggesting that the new creation through Jesus comes not by water and Spirit only, but also through blood.

In the first instance, though, John is talking about the incarnation and career of Jesus: he "came" by water and blood. That's a reference to the past life and work of Jesus, not a reference to his continuing work in the church. What is John referring to by "water and blood" and why does he emphasize that the Son came by both water and blood, not by water only? Jesus' ministry was framed by two baptisms, the water baptism where the Father identified him as Son (v. 9; cf. Matt. 3:17) and his blood baptism on the cross (cf. Mark 10:38–39). When James and John ask Jesus to give them places on his right and left in the kingdom, Jesus asks if they are capable of drinking the cup he needs to drink. They say yes, and then Jesus says: "You do not know what you ask. Are you able to drink the cup that I drink, and be baptized with the baptism that I am baptized with?" (Mark 10:38). Jesus' death was a baptism that fulfilled his water baptism, and his water baptism was a pointer to his coming baptism in blood.

We can get a sense of the polemical dimension of verse 6 if we remember what happened to Jesus at his baptism. That was the moment of his reception of the Spirit, and the Father's affirmation that he was the beloved Son. That is one of the ways he comes: through water, Spirit, and a Fatherly blessing from heaven. That way of coming was quite compatible with Jewish expectation. They wanted a Messiah who was anointed with the Spirit, a Messiah who heard voices from heaven, whose ministry was confirmed by signs from God. On the cross, all was different. No Spirit-dove descended, the skies grew dark and silent, Jesus cried out in the anguish of alienation from his Father. For Jews, this could be no messianic baptism. A messiah coming by water and Spirit, yes; a messiah coming by blood, no.

John proclaims a bloody messiah. A crucified messiah, Paul said, is a stumbling block for the Jews. It is an offense to the Greeks. A divine being coming through a baptism of water and Spirit might have made sense to the Greek mind. A hero who hears a voice from heaven made sense, but not a hero who was put to death on a cross. John proclaims a messiah who came by both water *and* blood, whose sonship is not only revealed at the ecstatic moment of baptism, but also, even supremely, in the slow death of crucifixion.

This gives us an insight into our experience as believers as well. We are called to follow and imitate the One who came by water and blood, not by water only, but by water and blood. There are moments of Spiritual ecstasy, there are highs in the Christian life, but we are called to bear witness even to death, to bear witness even with our blood. We are adopted into God's family by water; the Christian life is not by water only, but by water and blood.

John is also likely referring specifically to the moment of Jesus' death. When the soldier pierced Jesus' side, "water and blood" flowed out (John 19:34–35), and John not only notes this fact in his gospel, but emphasizes that he witnessed this happen. The words "witness," "water," and "blood" all appear here, just as in John 19. The water and blood that flowed from Jesus' side are witnesses to the identity of Jesus. He is the new Adam, birthing the church—the new Eve—from his side. He is the new Eden, which flowed with four rivers to the four points of the compass. He is the new rock in the wilderness, which gave water when struck to save the lives of Israel in the wilderness. He is the new glorified temple of Ezekiel, from which flowed water that renewed the ground (Ezekiel 47).[1] He is all this because he died on the cross, and from his side flowed blood and water. The life of Jesus is not confined to himself; it flows out to us.

This leads to verse 7, where John shifts the focus of attention. Verse 6 is about the "one who came," referring to the past event of Jesus' advent. But verse 6 doesn't talk about a past event, the "coming" of the Son, but about the continuing work of the Spirit. The Spirit "bears witness" (*martouroun*) in the present, long after Jesus died and rose again and ascended into heaven. Along with the Spirit there is water and blood in the church that bears witness to the presence and power of Jesus. John is referring to the water of baptism and the blood of the Lord's Supper. These are the continuing witnesses to Jesus in the church. Elsewhere, the "breaking of

---

1. In Ezekiel, the temple that flows with life-giving water is the temple restored after resurrection from exile. It may seem odd to connect this risen temple with the cross, but it is consistent with John's atonement theology, in which the cross is seen as Jesus' throne and crucifixion, his glorification.

bread" is shorthand for the Supper, but here, strangely, "blood" stands in for the whole rite. John has Jesus' own authority for this. He is talking about witnesses, and thus invoking a covenant-making setting, and Jesus makes it clear that the blood of the Supper is connected with the renewal of covenant (Matt. 26:28). The Spirit testifies to the new covenant flanked by the covenant witnesses of baptismal water and Eucharistic wine.[2]

These witnesses gain force through the work of the Spirit, who was given to Jesus at his baptism (John 1:32–34) and in whom he offered himself in sacrifice (cf. Heb. 9:14). The water of baptism and the blood of the Supper are effective witnesses to Jesus because the Spirit is at work in and through them. The witness of the Spirit can be trusted because the Spirit is truth (v. 6) and because the Spirit's witness is the witness of God (v. 9). We can put it this way, a bit pictorially but I think accurately: Jesus is filled with the Spirit at his baptism, but an anointed savior who does not release that Spirit to us does not give life, especially if he disappears from the scene, as Jesus does. If we are going to have life, the Spirit who is the Lord and Giver of life is going to have to be released to us. That is what happens on the cross. Before Jesus was struck with a spear and flowed with blood and water, John says that he "gave up" the Spirit, using a verb that can mean "to hand over" (John 19:30; the Greek verb is *paradidōmi*). John says Jesus lost the Spirit, a metaphor of death, but the wording suggests a passing-on of the Spirit. In his death, Jesus gave over the Spirit, and the centurion standing by immediately proclaimed Jesus "Son of God," the new imperial King. On the cross, Jesus flowed with Spirit as well as with blood and water. The Spirit burst out of the Spirit-filled Messiah.

It's not enough to have a Messiah who comes by water. He must come by water and blood. He can't just fill himself with the Spirit. That Spirit has to be released, and it's released when he dies

---

2. For more on the distinction of bread and wine in the Eucharist, see James B. Jordan, *From Bread To Wine*, available from Biblical Horizons, P.O. Box 1096, Niceville, florida, 32588.

and pours out blood and water. By his death, Jesus secures the Spirit for his people, as a continuing witness.

This is how we come to have life, John says in verses 11 and 12. When we trust God's witness in Spirit, water, and blood, we have the Son, and in having the Son we have life—eternal life. We don't have life unless we have the Son who is filled with the Spirit of life, and the only Son who has the Spirit of life is the Son who came by water and blood, not by water only. If we don't have the Son, if we don't have *this* Son, then we don't have life at all.

What Jesus gives us is eternal life. Of course, eternal life is not just a life of endless duration. Jesus says that eternal life consists in knowing the Father and his Son, Jesus Christ (cf. John 17:1–3). Eternal life describes a quality of life as much as the duration. We shouldn't ignore the point about duration. Eternal life is *more* than everlasting existence, but it *is* that.

Duration makes a difference. For many, life holds little joy because death always looms on the horizon. The fact that death is coming makes people frantic—they only have so much time to accomplish everything they want to accomplish, and are frustrated that time passes on without any concern for their hopes and dreams. If you live in fear of death, or in a frantic race to beat death by getting everything done before death comes, you don't really live at all (cf. v. 12). Those who trust in the witness of God have life—abundant life—in part because it stretches out endlessly. When we live in hope of an everlasting future life, we can live an abundant present life. When we have the Son and have eternal life, our death becomes only a moment in life; it's not the end, but a transition, a portal, a gateway to transformed renewed life, beyond anything we can ask or imagine. Death is incorporated as an experience of life, and this is what it means to live abundantly.

Cling to the Son, who is witnessed by the Spirit, water, and blood. Cling to the Son, and look ahead to a life that will never end.

CONFIDENCE IN PRAYER

Throughout his letter, John has been encouraging confidence, specifically confidence before God. He wants his readers to have confidence when Jesus comes, and tells his readers they can have confidence if they abide in Jesus: "Little children, abide in Him, so that when He appears, we may have confidence and not shrink away from Him in shame at His coming" (2:28). He urges them and us to love, because by loving, "we may have confidence in the day of judgment; because as He is, so also we are in the world" (4:17). Once earlier, he had tied confidence specifically to prayer: "If our heart does not condemn us, we have confidence before God; and whatever we ask we receive from Him, because we keep His commandments and do the things that are pleasing in His sight" (3:21–22).

John returns to this theme at the end of his letter, and specifically tells his readers how they can have confidence in prayer. He writes, he says, so that his readers can know they have eternal life, and so that this knowledge will in turn lead to confidence before God. Trusting in Jesus, we may be confident that our sins are forgiven and that we are acceptable to the Father. Also, trusting that Jesus is the Christ, the Son of God, makes us confident that the Father will listen to our prayers, and answer them (vv. 14–15).

John says some remarkable things about prayer here. Verse 14 repeats a promise reiterated frequently in the New Testament: "if we ask anything according to His will, He hears us." When John talks about "God's will," he is not talking directly about God's secret, decretal will that determines whatever comes to pass. He is not encouraging us to get a sneak peek at the decree so we can pray that God would do what he has eternally planned to do anyway. If we could do that, we could be very confident that God would answer; but we can't do that, and John isn't telling us to try. Rather, he is talking about God's revealed will, revealed in Jesus and in the Scriptures. If we pray in conformity to what God has promised and commanded in his word, we have confidence that he hears us. We don't need some special decretal knowledge to pray aright. God has told us everything we need to know in Scripture, and there are hundreds of revealed promises that we can pray back to God.

There's a sense, though, that the more deeply we know the revealed will of God, which is the revelation of God's own character, the closer we can come to anticipating God's secret will. Roommates who have lived together for years can anticipate how each will react in certain situations; wives can finish their husband's sentences, with great accuracy. How do they do that? They do it because they have developed an intimacy over many years, an intimacy that depends on conversations, common experiences, and mutual fellowship. Eventually, that intimacy goes beyond anything that has been talked about overtly. The intimacy between friends, siblings, husband and wife, becomes so close that each knows what the other will do or say in a situation they've never encountered before. We discern habits and patterns in the way our friends and spouses respond. My wife and I have never lost a child, but I have a sense of how she would react if we did.

As we become more intimately familiar with God's word in Scripture, we become more intimately familiar with God, his ways, his habits, his characteristic reactions. We can pray according to his will, finishing his sentences. This doesn't come from looking over God's shoulder, but from diligent study of Scripture, faithful participation in worship and sacraments, the usual means by which God reveals himself and his will to us.

Fundamentally, it comes by getting to know Jesus more and more intimately. Jesus is the Word of the Father, spoken eternally in the breath of the Spirit and now spoken at the end of the ages in the flesh. As the Word of the Father, the Son fully expresses the Father's will, desires, plans, and purposes. Jesus, as Athanasius often said, is the Will of the Father, and when we know Jesus we know something of what the Father is up to. In Jesus, the eternal decree of God and his revealed will meet. In Jesus, we know God as he shows himself, and know the God who was once hidden but is now revealed. We can pray with confidence because God has come into the open, as John says at the beginning of his letter. His will is evident not to some gnostic elite, or to some inner ring of priests, but to all who are anointed with the anointing from the Holy One.

The promise John repeats here holds whether our knowledge of God is mature or simple. The promise is that when we ask things in accord with the will of God, when we turn his promises into petitions, he hears us, and he answers us. This promise applies to *every* believer and to *everything* we pray for. Verse 15, if anything, makes an even more dramatic claim about our prayers: "if we know that he hears us whatever we ask, we know that we have." To simplify: if we know that he hears, we know that we have. God's hearing and our having are simultaneous. Knowing one means knowing the other. Knowing that God hears means knowing that we have. This means that as soon as God hears, we have; as soon as God listens, he gives. There is no lapse between request and gift as there is for us. God doesn't have to weigh options, think about it, get back to us. He doesn't have to wait and see how things turn out. There might be a time lapse between our request and the realization of the gift in our experience, but as soon as we know he hears our prayers according to his will, we also know we have it (not *will* have it, but *have* it).

With this promise, John encourages a particular attitude in prayer, and answers to it. A child asks for a particular Christmas present, and the parents have already bought it. He comes out on Christmas morning and looks around for the present he's sure is there somewhere. That's the way we ought to pray: when God hears, he gives, so we should be looking around every moment for the places where he has left the gifts he purchased, wrapped, and hid for us. The answers to our prayers are already ours, and they are out there in the future waiting for us. We just need to catch up to them. If we are praying according to the will of God, we ought to start each day looking under the tree for the answers to our prayers, in childlike confidence that "if we know he hears, we know we have." Our usual unbelieving tendency is to be shocked when prayers are answered. It would be wrong, but a better wrong, if we were disappointed and puzzled by unanswered prayer. We'd be more faithful if we were like the child on Christmas who can't understand why he didn't get what he asked for.

Of course, we sometimes, perhaps often, *don't* get just what we ask for. Sometimes what's lying out there in the future, wrapped up under the tree, is not what we expected. We look under the tree and there's a new sweater or a practical pair of mittens instead of the latest video game. That is not unusual, and how do we explain it? How is it consistent with this promise?

One part of the answer is that God remains sovereign. We don't control or manipulate God. If that's the only answer we give, however, we're in danger of nullifying the promise. We also have to add that what God pleases is precisely to do good for his people. What God desires is our salvation, our life, our fellowship with him. God desires all good for us, desires it far more deeply and perfectly than we ourselves desire it.

He knows far more perfectly and deeply exactly what we need. We have confidence in prayer because we know that God will give us what we ask or something better; he will give us just what we asked for, or something we need *more* than what we've asked for. We ask for a son, and we get a daughter, and we should conclude that God knew we needed a daughter more. We ask for peace and quiet, and God sends us a life-overturning trial. He knew peace would not have been good for us. We ask to be hired at a high salary at a prestigious law firm, but God knew that it would be better for us and for his kingdom if we ended up in a small firm writing wills for helpless old ladies. Our initial desires, our surface desires, our immediate requests may be denied. We may not get just what we ask, and we should be looking around eagerly for the things we actually need, the things that will actually be good for us.

The "problem" of "unanswered" prayer is partly the problem of our desires: we often don't know what we *want*, must less what we *need*. We don't know what we mean to pray for when we pray. God operates on us so that we learn to know what we want, and ask for it. Near the end of his most profound and beautiful book *Till We Have Faces*, C. S. Lewis's protagonist, Queen Orual, reflects on words:

Lightly men talk of saying what they mean. Often when he was teaching me to write in Greek the Fox would say, "Child, to say the very thing you really mean, the whole of it, nothing more or less or other than what you really mean; that's the whole art and joy of words." A glib saying. When the time comes to you at which you will be forced at last to utter the speech that has lain at the centre of your soul for years, which you have, all that time, idiot-like, been saying over and over, you'll not talk about joy of words. I saw well why the gods did not speak to us openly, nor let us answer. Till that word can be dug out of us, why should they hear the prattle that we think we mean? How can they meet us face to face till we have faces?

God puts us on the cross, tears and rends us, to dig out the word that we don't yet know we mean, to extract the prayer that we didn't think to pray. God grows us up until we ask for things that we really, most deeply, want.

SINS TO DEATH

Verse 16 seems to shift direction abruptly, but John is still talking about prayer, specifically prayer for a brother in sin. These verses are difficult, but there are some obvious things to notice. One of John's premises is that while all sin is unrighteousness, there are different sorts and degrees of sin. Further, it's obvious that we are supposed to respond to different sorts and degrees of sin in different ways. Some people have a "sin is sin is sin" attitude. There's certainly truth to that, as John acknowledges. However, if we don't recognize distinctions among sins, we're liable to be harsh and judgmental and uncharitable. For some Christians, any small infraction becomes an unforgivable sin.

John applies his promises regarding prayer to a specific situation. We should pray for brothers who are in sin, and "God will to him give life" (v. 16). In the Greek, the wording is more ambiguous. John says, "If anyone sees his brother sinning a sin not unto death, he will ask and he will give life" (1 John 5:16). There is no stated subject for the verb "give." Some commentators suggest a change of subject in the main clause: the brother "asks" but God "gives life." That's grammatically awkward, and Stott bites the bullet to say that John is attributing a life-giving efficacy to our prayers. Obviously, God is the one who ultimately gives life, but God gives life through our prayers and mediation: "under God, he who asks life for a brother may be said not just to gain it for him but actually to 'give' it to him."[3] The righteous man, the proverb says, is a tree of life, and the prayers of the righteous man are the fruit on that tree.[4]

This is a remarkable promise: like Jesus the Advocate (2:1), we have the privilege of interceding for our brothers. He is the firmament between the Father and the creation, but we are "in" the firmament, part of the sapphire pavement beneath the feet of our Father. Through our prayers, God gives life and forgiveness of sins to others. Through the Spirit of Jesus, the church has the power to bind and loose, to forgive and retain sins (cf. John 21:19–23). This also implies that we all share responsibility for one another's sins. Our tendency, sinful and modern, is often to leave one another alone. If we see someone doing something we don't like, we withdraw, keep our distance, and move away. It's *his* problem, not ours. We don't want to take any responsibility for the sins of our brothers. That's not the portrait of life in the church that John gives. He tells us that we are to pray for one another when we "see" someone in sin. We should take that as our responsibility. Elsewhere, the New Testament makes it clear that we are to intervene to correct a sinning brother. Jesus said that if our brother sins against us, we should rebuke him, and Paul says that "those who are spiritual" are called to correct and restore Christians who are wandering (Matt. 5; 18; Gal. 6:1).

John tells us about the prior response: prayer. If some Christians back away and avoid brothers who are in sin, others are only

---

3. Stott, *Letters*, loc. cit.

4. James 5:20 says something similar: the "turning" of the sinner is attributed to human intervention, and the soul that is saved, whether it is the soul of the sinner or the one who intervenes, is saved by human action.

too willing to jump in and correct everything they see that seems slightly off. John offers a good rule of thumb: don't correct *any* brother concerning his sin if you haven't *first* prayed for his sin. Even when correction happens, it should happen *prayerfully*.

What does John mean by "sins to death" and "sins not to death"? John's distinction is rooted in the Old Testament distinction between inadvertent sins (Lev. 4:2, 13, 22, 27; 5:15–18) and intentional sins. Inadvertencies could be removed by sacrifice, but high-handed sins were punished with exile or death (Num. 15:30–31; Deut. 17:12). The law also makes it clear that even high-handed sins can be cleansed by sacrifice *if* they are confessed. Confession, as it were, reduces highhanded sins to inadvertencies, which can be removed by sacrifice. Jesus offered the final sacrifice, and John indicates (1:8–10) that the efficacy of the sacrifice applies to our sins when we confess.

This is why we confess our sins every Lord's Day in worship, and why we frequently confess even those sins that we cannot know or understand: "Cleanse me from hidden faults," David prays. John's words are also an encouragement to be open in confessing sin to God and, when necessary, to one another. We are reluctant to confess, out of pride, concern for our reputation, desire for respect. We want to maintain a front and put on a good show. Refusing to confess sin is deadly, because no sacrifice will remove a high-handed sin that is not confessed. Achan confessed his sin only after he was caught, and he was buried under a pile of stones. Saul offered a kind of confession, but only after he had tried to shift blame to the people; and he lost the kingdom and crown.

In the context, John has his opponents in view, those who "went out from us" (2:19). He is referring to the false teachers who have not only left the apostolic fellowship, teaching without apostolic authority, but have also abandoned faith in Jesus. They revert to the elementary principles of the world, and thereby commit a sin unto death (cf. Matt. 12:31–32; Heb. 6:4–6). Those who have been in the New Covenant—who have tasted the gifts of God and the fruits of Christ's work and given up those gifts, who have shared in the Spirit and then spurned the Spirit, who have confessed Jesus and then turned from Jesus and become his enemies—these cannot be renewed, and John says we ought not to pray for them. (John does not explicitly prohibit prayer, but that is the tenor of the passage.)

John seems harsh, but there is ample biblical precedent for this. God himself tells people to stop praying at various places in the Old Testament. There comes a time when the right thing to do is to *stop* praying. According to 1 Samuel 3:14, the sins of the house of Eli are so flagrant, so in-your-face, that God is determined to destroy his house: "I have sworn to the house of Eli that the iniquity of Eli's house shall not be atoned for by sacrifice or offering forever." Jeremiah is told several times not to pray. "Do not pray for this people," the Lord tells him after instructing the prophet to preach in the temple, "and do not lift up a cry or prayer for them, and do not intercede with Me, for I do not hear you" (7:16). Again, "Do not pray for this people, nor lift up a cry or prayer for them; for I will not listen when you call to Me because of their disaster" (11:14). Because Israel loves to wander, and does not keep their feet in check, "Do not pray for the welfare of this people" (14:11).

John is not talking about those who drift and wander. He is not talking about Christians who slip into sin or into a lifestyle they should leave behind. Sins of weakness are not high-handed sins, and such believers can be recovered. He is talking about apostate false teachers, who consciously and deliberately turn from Jesus and become the opponents of Jesus and his people. And he's saying that we should not pray for God to forgive them and give them life. "Do not pray for this people," as Yahweh told Jeremiah.

John concludes his first epistle with a series of reminders of what we know. Three times he uses the verb "we know." We know that those who are born of God, however, do not commit this deadly sin (v. 18), because the Lord guards them from Satan. We know that we are from God, and have been delivered from Satan, who controls the "world"—the world of Judaism specifically (cf. John 8:44). We know that Jesus has come, to give us understanding, and to give us eternal life. This is the sum and substance of John's letter. God is the life-giver, and he has come out of hiding and sent the Word of Life into the world that we might have life, abundantly. If we want life, eternal life, we must cling to him. As the life-giver, he is the true God, and all alternatives are idols (v. 21). So, keep yourselves from idols.

11

To the Chosen Lady
2 John 1–13

2 John 1:1The elder to the elect lady and her children, whom I love in truth, and not only I, but also all who know the truth, ²because of the truth that abides in us and will be with us forever: ³Grace, mercy, and peace will be with us, from God the Father and from Jesus Christ the Father's Son, in truth and love.

⁴I rejoiced greatly to find some of your children walking in the truth, just as we were commanded by the Father. ⁵And now I ask you, dear lady—not as though I were writing you a new commandment, but the one we have had from the beginning— that we love one another. ⁶And this is love, that we walk according to his commandments; this is the commandment, just as you have heard from the beginning, so that you should walk in it. ⁷For many deceivers have gone out into the world, those who do not confess the coming of Jesus Christ in the flesh. Such a one is the deceiver and the antichrist. ⁸Watch yourselves, so that you may not lose what we have worked for, but may win a full re-

ward. ⁹Everyone who goes on ahead and does not abide in the teaching of Christ, does not have God. Whoever abides in the teaching has both the Father and the Son. ¹⁰If anyone comes to you and does not bring this teaching, do not receive him into your house or give him any greeting, ¹¹for whoever greets him takes part in his wicked works.

¹²Though I have much to write to you, I would rather not use paper and ink. Instead I hope to come to you and talk face to face, so that our joy may be complete.

¹³The children of your elect sister greet you.

2 John has a fairly clear structure. John begins and ends with greetings to "chosen" ladies (*eklektē*) and to children (*tekna*), and within the inclusio, the structure is roughly chiastic:

A. Greeting to the chosen Lady and children, vv. 1–3
  B. Commandment to love, vv. 4–6
    C. Deceivers and antichrist, vv. 7–8
  B′ Abide in teaching, vv. 9–11
A′ Greeting from children to chosen sister, vv. 12–13

The letter centers on the warning about antichrists who deny that Jesus came in the flesh, and who are leading people astray from the teaching of Christ. The B section is itself a clear chiasm:

A. Children walking in truth, v. 4a
  B. Commandment from Father, v. 4b
    C. Old commandment to love, v. 5
    C′ Love is keeping commandments, v. 6a
  B′ Commandment from the beginning, v. 6b
A′ Walk in it, v. 6c

From this outline, it is clear that 2 John covers many of the same themes as 1 John, and is evidently written by the same writer. Many of the same phrases and terms are used: the "new commandment" to love (vv. 5–6; 1 John 2:7–11); the danger from "deceivers" and "antichrist" (v. 7; 1 John 2:18–19; 4:1–6); the confession that "Jesus Christ came in the flesh" (v. 7; 1 John 4:2); instructions about how to treat apostate false teachers (vv. 10–11; 1 John 5:15–17). Many of these themes are also emphasized in John's gospel, which indicates that the author of this letter is John, the apostle of Jesus and the author of the Fourth Gospel.

Not only does this letter use many of the same phrases and terms, but John is dealing with the same crisis situation that he faced in 1 John. Deceivers have gone out into the world, and the deceivers are threatening to mislead the church. This is the same crisis situation that Jesus had predicted in the Olivet Discourse, the deceivers who would mislead even the elect, if that were possible. The time is getting short before the destruction of Jerusalem and its temple by the Romans. Persecution is intense, and heresies are abounding. The deceivers are already in the world, and believers must "watch yourselves" to keep from losing what has been given already.

Though John is dealing with the same crisis, he addresses the church and identifies himself in a way that he did not in 1 John. In 1 John, John doesn't identify himself at all. The letter simply begins with an announcement of the Word of Life who has made himself visible and audible and tangible in the world. In 2 John, though, John identifies himself and the recipient of the letter. He writes as an elder (*presbuteron*) to the "chosen Lady." The Greek for "chosen lady" is *eklektē kuria*. Some believe that John is writing to a specific woman, perhaps named "Eclecta" and perhaps named "Kuria." But that doesn't fit with the way John writes the letter. John uses plural verbs (vv. 6, 8, 10) and plural pronouns (v. 8), so it's clear that he's writing to a group. Moreover, the letter ends with reference to another Eclecta, a sister (v. 13). It would be odd if two sisters were both named Eclecta.

Instead, the "lady" is a church, and the fact that the Lady has a sister shows that he's talking not about the church as a whole, the universal or catholic church, but about a specific local congregation who is part of a family of chosen women. The church is the "elect" or chosen (v. 1) bride of the Lord Jesus (Eph. 5:22–33). More specifically, John speaks of the church as the mother of her members as Paul does in Galatians (Gal. 5:26). It's fitting for John to address a church as "Lady," using the feminine form of the word "Lord." The church has a Lord, Jesus, and the church herself is the Lady, who rules and reigns and shares a house with her Lord. Jesus is a king, and he has a queen—his people.

It's worth noticing how John uses the word "elect" here. At times, the Bible speaks of the people who have been elect before the foundations of the world, as Paul does in Ephesians 1. God has chosen a people, a bride, before the world ever existed, and precisely those people, that bride, will enjoy the consummation of the marriage with Jesus in the final heavens and earth. Here John is not using the word that way. This Lady is a specific congregation (who has a sister, perhaps many sisters), and this specific church is under threat and needs to be admonished and instructed. This church is the church in history. John doesn't know for sure that every member of this church is going to be with God forever. From his first letter, it is clear that he is aware that some "go out" from the church who are not of the church. He doesn't know that everyone in the family of the Lady are eternally chosen. Yet, he addresses the whole church as the "chosen Lady," the Lady who shares with the Lord. In short, the Bible doesn't reserve the language of "election" for those who are elect before the foundation of the world. The whole church is the "chosen Lady" of the Lord. The opening verses thus set up a typological picture of the condition of the church.

The church is a Lady, and this Lady faces threats from deceivers. As elder, John is the guardian and protector for the Lady, keeping her from being deceived and hoping for a time when he can see her face-to-face. John is evoking the situation in Eden: the church is the new Lady Eve, faced by the Antichrist deceiver, the Satanic tempter and accuser, and the elder is a faithful Adam who is guarding her by his words and warnings against the deceivers. As a servant to the Last Adam, John plays an Adamic role. Every church has this same typological structure. Every church is a lady of Lord Jesus, a new Eve. Every church has "children" that are the members of the church. The pastor and elders of the church are supposed to imitate the true Bridegroom, Jesus, who gave up his life rather than let his bride be seduced by deceivers.

This typology fits the grand scheme of John's work as a whole. His gospel and Revelation fit together as a single two-volume work. The two books are united by the story of the Lord and his bride. Jesus is identified as the Bridegroom at the beginning of John's gospel (John 2), and early in John's gospel, he meets a woman at the well and talks to her about her marriages (John 4). Yet that woman is not his bride. Jesus meets Mary in the garden after his resurrection (John 19), and yet Mary is not his bride. In Revelation, there is a prominent harlot, the city identified as Babylon, but of course she is no true bride (John 17–18). It's not until we get to the end of the book of Revelation that Jesus' bride is revealed as the New Jerusalem that descends from heaven (John 19–21). Here in 2 John, John anticipates the revelation of that glorious Lady. This Lady descends from heaven, made the Bride spotless and without wrinkle or blemish, because Jesus preserves her from defilement, through the warnings of John and other elders and apostles.

John warns that the Lady and her children will not be ready to meet her husband when he appears (cf. Matt. 25): "Watch yourselves, that you might not lose what we have accomplished, but that you may receive a full reward" (v. 8). It's possible that the Lady, or her children, might fall away. Verse 4 implies that some already have: if "some" are walking in the truth, what about the "others"? If they join the deceivers, they might lose what has been achieved, and they would not receive the reward that comes at the consummation.

John gives several instructions to the Lady to preserve her for the coming of her husband. First, John reiterates the points he made about obeying the commandments of God in his first letter. The chief commandment is the command to love one another (v. 5), and John is happy to know that some of the church's children are doing just this (v. 4). The command to love is the pathway for life, and we are called to walk on the pathway set out from the beginning (v. 6). This commandment is the command to love one another, but it's also the command to believe in the Lord Jesus, as we learned from 1 John. The Lady is preserved in the path of life by trusting Jesus and by living out of that trust in love for one another. Second, John is particularly concerned with the threat that comes from false teachers. Along this pathway of loving obedience and obedient love are brigands, the deceivers who threaten to plot to waylay the children who travel on it. The threat doesn't come from individuals who hold false beliefs, but from false teachers who propagate heresy (v. 10). He tells the Lady ahead of time that deceivers are out there, threatening her children and trying to get her and them off the path of truth and the way of the commandments. Knowing ahead of time, they can be prepared to resist the deceivers.

Third, they have to keep their distance from the deceivers. John forbids the Lady from welcoming false teachers into the "house" of the church (v. 10) and from giving these teachers a blessing and greeting (v. 11). This is consistent with the command to love: true love guards the beloved from error, a true Adam kicks the serpent out of the garden. John is not prohibiting us from welcoming heretics and false believers and unbelievers into our homes, and having private conversations with them. He's not saying that we should slam the door in the faces of the Jehovah's Witnesses or Mormons who come to the door.

Far from prohibiting us from befriending and showing hospitality to unbelievers, the New Testament encourages us to show hospitality to unbelievers. There is a priority to brothers and sisters, but we are to "do good to all men," Paul says, "especially those of the household of faith." We are to "show hospitality to strangers," we're told in Hebrews 13. But we should not encourage the teaching of false teachers, give them a platform in the church, or give them the approval of an official greeting. We are to love them, but we are to love them in a way that aims to turn them from their false teaching and leads to repentance.

John ends his letter expressing hope that he will see the chosen Lady face-to-face, and not have to communicate by ink and paper. Though John is talking about a personal visit to the church, the language is rich with associations of Jesus' coming. Now, Paul says, we see through a glass darkly; now our Lord communicates with his Lady through the love letter that is the Bible. He communicates with us through ink and paper in order to preserve us faithful until the time when he will unveil his face, and we shall be like him, for we shall see him as he is. John invokes this promise by speaking of his own coming as an apostolic parousia, when he will address his chosen Lady in his own voice rather than through the mediation of ink and paper.[1]

This is the way that the chosen Lady of John's letter—or any church—can remain on the path, retain what has been accomplished, and receive the reward that is promised at the coming of her husband. She must remain on the path of truth and the way of God's commandments; she must be aware that deceivers lie in wait to take us from that way; and she must avoid giving false teachers any approval or welcome. In this way, the Lord preserves his Bride, and keeps her until the glorious consummation, when she will enter the bridal chamber to see him face-to-face.

---

1. Thanks to James Jordan for this way of putting it.

12

IMITATE THE GOOD
3 John 1–14

3 John 1:1The elder to the beloved Gaius, whom I love in truth.
²Beloved, I pray that all may go well with you and that you may
be in good health, as it goes well with your soul. ³For I rejoiced
greatly when the brothers came and testified to your truth, as in-
deed you are walking in the truth. ⁴I have no greater joy than to
hear that my children are walking in the truth.

⁵Beloved, it is a faithful thing you do in all your efforts for
these brothers, strangers as they are, ⁶who testified to your love
before the church. You will do well to send them on their journey
in a manner worthy of God. ⁷For they have gone out for the sake
of the name, accepting nothing from the Gentiles. ⁸Therefore we
ought to support people like these, that we may be fellow workers for the truth.

⁹I have written something to the church, but Diotrephes, who
likes to put himself first, does not acknowledge our authority.
¹⁰So if I come, I will bring up what he is doing, talking wicked

nonsense against us. And not content with that, he refuses to welcome the brothers, and also stops those who want to and puts them out of the church.

¹¹Beloved, do not imitate evil but imitate good. Whoever does good is from God; whoever does evil has not seen God. ¹²Demetrius has received a good testimony from everyone, and from the truth itself. We also add our testimony, and you know that our testimony is true.

¹³I had much to write to you, but I would rather not write with pen and ink. ¹⁴I hope to see you soon, and we will talk face to face.

¹⁵Peace be to you. The friends greet you. Greet the friends, every one of them.

John is a true apostolic pastor. He has a ministry that covers the entire church; a ministry to specific congregations, and a ministry to individual believers. His gospel is addressed to the entire church, and the Revelation is, in an important sense, a series of letters from Jesus to the entire world. His epistles, however, display his interest in individual churches and congregations, as they progressively narrow their focus. His first letter addresses the universal church (1 John). While John may be dealing with issues in a particular congregation, the letter is broadly addressed to believers in general. The "chosen Lady" of 2 John is not an individual but a specific congregation. 3 John is addressed to an individual Christian, Gaius, and this letter also speaks of other individuals. Compared with the other epistles of John, 3 John is full of names: Gaius (v. 1), Diotrephes (v. 9), Demetrius (v. 12), and twice he uses the word "name" (*onoma*, vv. 7, 14).

The letter as a whole has a neatly-chiastic structure:

A. Greeting to Gaius, v. 1
  B. Beloved, gladness in witness, vv. 2–4
    C. Beloved, faithfulness to strangers, vv. 5–8
      D. Diotrephes loves to be first, vv. 9–10
    C' Beloved, do what is good, v. 11
  B' Demetrius has a good witness, v. 12
A' Greeting to friends by name, vv. 13–14

John is not content with speaking to crowds, not content to preach from a safe distance. He also encourages, rebukes, and exhorts *individuals*. He addresses the church as a whole as "beloved" (1 John 2:7; 4:1, 7), professes his love for the chosen Lady (2 John 1), and also addresses the individual Gaius as "beloved" (3 John 1). His love for the church is general, but it is also personal and specific. John is not one with only a catholic love for the church, but no concern with the particular persons who make up the church. He serves the church by serving individuals and congregations; he serves individuals and congregations by serving the universal church.

John's interest in individuals and individual churches is not a passing interest. He is intensely interested in the doings of individuals and congregations, just as Paul was. John writes here to Gaius, but we find in the third epistle that he had already written a letter concerning the situation with Diotrephes. Diotrephes ignored that letter (v. 9), but John didn't just back off and let things go. He didn't throw up his hands and say, well, nothing we can do there. He pursued the situation with a second letter, this one to Gaius, and with a hope of a personal visit (vv. 13–14).

The rich diversity of John's pastoral work is important not only in the church but in Christian living as a whole. You can't deal with your family in the aggregate. Family worship is great, but parents need to love and guide and train each child individually. You can't deal with a business as a bunch of faceless cogs in the machine. Some memos go to the whole company. Some memos have to be more narrowly construed and go to a single person. In whatever leadership position you find yourself, you have to engage with this range of pastoral contexts: the group as a whole, subgroups within, and individuals.

HOSPITALITY

John addresses a conflict in Gaius's church centering on proper treatment of strangers and visitors, especially the question of how traveling Christians are received when they visit other churches.

John commends Gaius because he acts faithfully in receiving strangers and sending them "on their way in a manner worthy of God" (vv. 5–6). Diotrophes, by contrast, does not receive the brothers and prevents others from doing so (v. 10). From the time of Jesus' earthly ministry, receiving messengers from Jesus is equivalent to receiving Jesus (cf. Matt. 10:11–15). When the Twelve were sent out during Jesus' lifetime, he sent them out as his representatives. When a town or home welcomed the apostles in, they were receiving Jesus himself in a very practical way. They were showing their faith in the gospel of the kingdom, and their support for the mission of Jesus. At times, receiving missionaries represented a real risk, since the Jews were hostile to anyone who supported Jesus. Receiving missionaries was an act of courageous faith.

More broadly, our treatment of Jesus' disciples and "brothers" is the key demonstration of our reception of Jesus. In the judgment scene in Matthew 25, the nations are judged by their treatment of the naked, poor, hungry, sick, and imprisoned. If they clothe the naked, give to the poor, feed the hungry, minister to the sick, visit the imprisoned, they are judged as sheep. If they fail, they are judged as goats. As Jesus closes this parable, it becomes clear that he's not talking about treatment of the poor and naked and hungry in general. Of course, we should be generous in every direction, but the specific standard is the treatment of "the least of *these my brothers*" (25:40). Anyone who has clothed, fed, or visited a brother of Jesus has "done it to Me," Jesus says. In this sense, every member of Jesus' family, which means every believer, is a representative of Christ. What people do to Christians is what they do to Christ, since we are members of his body, since we are, together with Jesus, "Christ," the Anointed One (1 Cor. 12:12).

The missionaries receive nothing, John says, from "Gentiles" (v. 7). He is talking about those outside the church, but he calls them Gentiles because the church is the community of the true Israel, the true Jews. This is one of many signs in the New Testament that the church is the continuation of Israel, the renewed people of God. The lines of humanity have been redrawn. In Christ, the nations are reunited. Babel is reversed, because Jesus broke the dividing wall that separated Jews and Gentiles. Contrary to some liberal theologies, this doesn't mean there are *no* boundaries in the New Covenant. Though the new Israel is made up of people from every tribe and tongue and nation, there are still boundaries between Israel and the Gentiles.

John emphasizes that instead of relying on outsiders for support, the missionaries receive help from the members of the church. Many missionaries end up, by necessity or choice, depending on outside work for their practical support. That's what Paul did, working as a tentmaker as he traveled from place to place. That is an honorable practice. But the New Testament also shows us that missionaries are funded and supported by churches. In Matthew 10, the disciples are supported by the people they minister to. In 3 John, and in some places in Paul, the support apparently comes from other Christians who are not necessarily part of the church that is being ministered to. Gaius receives missionaries from somewhere else, and supports them at least to that extent.

John also has some encouraging things to say to those who are not actually traveling as missionaries. Sometimes Christians feel as if they are left out of the whole enterprise of spreading the gospel when they can't go onto the mission field, and some teachers and missionaries are only too willing to make believers feel guilty for their failure to venture out. It would be wrong, of course, to resist a real call to spread the gospel in other places, but staying home doesn't mean that we are not involved in the mission of the church. John describes those who support missionaries, like Gaius, as co-workers with missionaries (v. 8). Not everyone is called to missions, but even those who remain at home are laborers as they support missionaries through prayers, hospitality, and financial support.

In Gaius's church, the overt conflict is about the support and reception of strangers who arrive in the church, but the real problem is different. John says that the key problem with Diotrephes is that he is proud, that he wants to be first among the brothers. The real problem is the ambition of Diotrephes. With regard to missions, this expresses itself in Diotrephes' refusal to receive the brothers who come to the church. The reasons are obscure, but the fact of it is clear. Gaius welcomes strangers who are also brothers; Diotrephes does not. And he goes even further, threatening to throw those who support traveling missionaries out of the church (v. 10). Diotrephes apparently has some authority in the church, or else his threats wouldn't mean much. John is dealing with a leader in the church who refuses to receive the traveling brothers and wants everyone else to follow his example. He's willing to use strong-arm tactics to get his way, and to make sure that the brothers are not received.

We might get some sense of his motivation by looking at what else John says about him. His lust for supremacy reveals itself in unjust accusations, wicked words, refusal to receive missionaries, and excommunication of anyone who doesn't follow his instructions (v. 10). He refuses to accept the apostles, or their exhortations and rebukes (v 9). John has written to him once before and it has not had any effect. It seems that Diotrephes refuses the missionaries precisely because they come representing the apostles, whose authority Diotrephes won't accept. Such behavior should have no place in the church, whose Lord humbled himself and placed his people ahead of himself. John does not hesitate to say that people like Diotrephes are "evil" and that they have "not seen God" (v. 11). God gives generously, and is merciful. Anyone who acts like a Diotrephes doesn't know God as he ought.

Though the specific situation of Gaius' church is not replicated in every church, the threat of prideful members and leaders like Diotrephes is a perpetual threat. John instructs churches of all times to pay attention and watch out for men in the church who lust for leadership. Watch out for the ambitious man. Watch out for the men who refuse to bow before authority, take advice and counsel, resist necessary rebukes and exhortations. Watch out for the men and women in the church who fill the church with gossip and evil words about the leaders of the church. Watch out for people, John says, who refuse to receive brothers, who close themselves off from Christians who are not part of the in-group. Watch out for these Judaizing tendencies.

This is all the product of pride, of wishing to be first, and it destroys the fellowship of the church. This is evil conduct of the most serious nature. If we are going to be judged by how we treat the "least of these my brothers," then we had better be very careful to avoid pride, ambition, gossip, slander, evil words, and resistance to counsel. We ought instead to be cultivating humility, service, edifying speech, and submission to the authority of those who are set over us.

What is the solution to pride and its destructive effects on the church? Surely, listening to the rebukes of the wise is essential. John points to something else as well. The church is not only a place of words and teaching. The church is a school, but not *only* a school. Perhaps better, schools are not places where we only learn from the words spoken by the teacher. John says that we will be formed in humility by imitation of the humble. Imitation is inherent in human life. We learn to speak by imitation, and many of our other habits are picked up from others. We are made to imitate, to be like another, because we are made in the image of God. You know this from your own life and, if you have children, from watching your children. Your hand gestures, ways of speaking, ways of walking, postures, accents, and much else about you is borrowed from parents, teachers, close friends, and other models. Some members of my family unconsciously change their accent depending on whom they're talking to. Or think of how often you see your own behavior replicated in your children, for good or bad.

John says that the same phenomenon exists in the church. We need *teaching* about righteousness and holiness, but also need incarnate models of doing good, models we can imitate. This is one of the reasons it's so crucial for healthy Christian living that we become participants in a family of believers, a local church. You can sit at home listening to sermons on CD or radio; you can serve yourself communion with crackers and grape juice from the kitchen. But you can't get models of Christian living to imitate without being with other Christians. You can say "I am imitating Christ, not any Christian," but Paul says, "Be imitators of *me*, as I am an imitator of Christ" (1 Cor. 11:1).

This of course lays great responsibility on parents, elders, and adult members of the church to live faithfully. People do watch. People do imitate what you do. Make sure that what they see in your behavior is a display of the righteousness of Christ, the faith and faithfulness of Jesus.

This is the way the church will avoid the conflicts and chaos created by men like Diotrephes. The church needs faithful teaching, but also faithful living. The church needs mature models for others to imitate. The church needs men and women who are humble, who speak to edify the body, who demonstrate hospitality even to strangers, who are generous. The members of the church need to find such men and women and imitate their faithfulness. The solution to church conflicts is for everyone to follow John's exhortation: "Do not imitate what is evil, but what is good."

In the end, John's letters circle back to the beginning. We are to imitate what is good, and who is good but God alone? God has demonstrated his goodness in speaking the Word of Life into the world, so that he might be seen, heard, touched, and handled. God the Light has come out from the shadows to judge and give life. That is the gospel that the Gnosticizing Jews and Judaizing Gnostics refuse to hear and believe, but that is the gospel that we are to imitate, as we shine with the Light of the Spirit in us, imitating Jesus and letting our light shine before men that they may see our works and glorify our Father, the Father of lights.